SOVIET BONDAGE

SEQUEL TO "RED EXODUS"

by

MAYME SEVANDER

Mayme Sevander

OSCAT

OF SOVIET BONDAGE

Distributed by Brooks Anderson
2939 Lake Avenue South • Duluth, MN 55802 • U.S.A.
Library of Congress Cataloging-in-Publication Data
DK 34.A45 S 49 1996
ISBN 1-887801-53-7

Line art illustrations by Andrei Feldshteyn

Edited by Elizabeth Icks and Julie Ahasay

Design, layout & production by Kollath Graphic Design, Duluth
Printed by McNaughton & Gunn, Saline, Michigan.

Cover photograph: a 1935 high school class at the Finnish school in Petrozavodsk. Most of the students are Americans.

Row 1 (from left to right) Viola Sandros, Aino Forsten (principal), Alice Välimaa, Grigori Makarov, Maila Eklund.

Row 2 Santeri Voinov, Erkki Puustinen, Tatyana Ananina, George Hiltunen, Toivo Paaso, Oiva Laakso, Arnold Pilppola, Kerttu Viljanen, Kirillova.

Row 3 Ernest Niva, Uuno Mäki, Ivan Yegorov, Pauli Seppanen, Onni Björn, Pauli Yakovlev, girl's name forgotten, Fred Henrickson, Irja Ryömänen.

To the memory of our parents and peers
whose lives were cut short by Stalinist tyranny.
To our offspring who hopefully will remember
and never find themselves in idealist quandary.

"Experience Teaches Slowly and at the Cost of Mistakes."

—James Anthony Froude

ACKNOWLEDGEMENTS

Acknowledgements are due foremostly to FINLANDIA FOUNDATION TRUST and FINLANDIA FOUNDATION, Inc., whose grant made it possible for me to go on with research on Finnish-American emigration from the United States and Canada to Russia and publish this sequel to "Red Exodus." I lack words to express my gratitude.

But for the moral support, initiative and persistence of friends on the East Coast Joyce and Lloyd Hannula and Martha Bradshaw I'd have never applied for the grant. So they too have my heartfelt thanks.

Throughout the years I've had the inestimable support of College of St. Scholastica (Duluth) Dr. Al Nephew as counselor and computer wizard. Without him I'd have been lost. As usual, Rev. Brooks Anderson and his wife Coral welcomed me back Home and made their computer facilities available until I got settled down with my own. Thank you, dear friends!

My first reader, critic and editor was Elizabeth Icks from CSS, Duluth. Her profound knowledge and interest in the subject under consideration made the observations valuable. I thank her for efficiency and speed.

Personal thanks go to Aili R. Bell, Alexandria, VA, for her interest in my project and the idea on the Winter War poems. Robert Taylor (Switzerland), Viola Sandros (Germany) and Thelma Skinkis (Sweden) had the patience to maintain a lively and productive correspondence with the author. Irma Janhunen, Miriam and Elmer Nousiainen (Petrozavodsk) gave unstintingly of their time. They all have my warmest thanks. Also thanks go to Julie Ahasay for editing and proofreading assistance.

Rick Kollath and his team worked magic with the layout. Their advice and efforts enabled me to meet the deadlines! Thank you, Rick!

Thanks are also due to Petrozavodsk University with whose help I finally got access to archives of Republic Karelia and the Karelian NKVD. The personnel of these organizations were extremely helpful and I owe them a "thank-you"!

Regardless of the help of all these wonderful people mistakes are bound to have crept in and there's no one to blame but myself. I'll appreciate any corrections and proposals.

CONTENTS

Introduction

Three years have passed since the publication of "Red Exodus." I presume the reader of this sequel is acquainted with the first two books, as this is not a reiteration of familiar facts, although now and then you'll encounter names you've read before. I was compelled to go on, as "Red Exodus" was written without archive materials of any kind and the very process of writing kept raising questions like, Who were the emigrants whom I hadn't found up to date? How many of them were there all in all? What had happened to them? Only documents would serve to provide answers to these seemingly simple questions, which in reality were extremely complex: so much water had flown under the bridge—60 years and more. A sense of unrest kept gnawing at my heart: would there actually be papers throwing light on these issues? Petrozavodsk was, after all, occupied by forces of Finland's army for almost three years. Had it been possible to save documents? If so, what state would they be in? Would they be readable?

Upon returning to Petrozavodsk in December 1993, I finally got to the Karelian Republican Archives (KRA). I was actually invited there, probably as a result of a published interview in which I complained of not having had access to documents connected with my research. I plunged into work without delay.

It's only natural that many documents were missing and some were in such disorder that you could only make them out with a magnifying glass. But there they were! Leafing through one of the files on the very first day my attention was riveted to a paper signed by Oscar Corgan with some writing in backhand on it. It sure was exciting to recognize my own childish hand! (I was in the habit of going to Dad's office on 126th St., New York, straight from school to help him with paper work). A mental vision of Father in his grey sweater bent over masses of paper littering the desk and an adolescent blond-as-could-be girl sitting not far from him flashed through my mind. It brought tears to my eyes.

The first months of work with the KRA papers made it clear that without the NKVD (People's Commissariat of Internal Affairs) files many a question would remain unanswered. Petrozavodsk University, where I had taken up my usual teaching job, provided me with recommendations stressing that papers concerning the purges were a must for my research, as hundreds of Finnish-Americans had shared the lot of thousands of other victims in Karelia. So already in March 1994, I tackled the papers of the NKVD Archives (NKVDA).

Now the index I had compiled on the basis of letters and interviews served a good purpose: it eased orientation in both archives, it helped to verify facts rendered in the stories of the victims' families. But that was not all: I found hundreds of new names and facts which will be dealt with on these pages.

By early 1996 I had several documents in which to check on data concerning the Finnish-American emigrants;

1. My basic index. The initial one, a third of which was published at the end of "Red Exodus," was incomplete. Introducing new names and data and correcting mistakes that had crept in were made easier.

2. Lists of returnees (the lucky ones, whose names will not figure on these pages).

3. A list of immigrants who had died natural deaths.

4. Names of rehabilitated persons from the journal "Carelia."

5. Names of rehabilitated persons from the newspaper "Petrozavodsk."

6. Names of persons arrested and sentenced (NKVDA).

7. Sentences put into effect (NKVDA).

8. Passenger lists of groups that arrived from America to Russia in 1930–34. Some are still lacking and the whole set remains to be established. Only findings in the US and Canada will enable me to amass the whole set.

Emigration to the Soviet Union occurred either directly from Finland or from the US and Canada. The majority of grown-ups from America were also Finland-born but the circumstances of their emigration differed.

Petrozavodsk researcher Eila Lahti-Argutina has for several years been doing substantial work along the lines of emigration from Finland, so hopefully, our joint efforts will help to answer the questions stated above.

The passenger lists were essential in determining whether this or that person had arrived to Karelia from America or from Finland. Data on a person in the "Carelia" lists contained only the birthplace, which, naturally, and in most cases, was Finland. Upon finding the name of an emigre from Canada or the US in the NKVDA papers among the "loikkarit" ("border hoppers"—illegal border crossers), I had to return to the names of hundreds of others to verify who they were in reality. Thus I found almost a hundred American Finns among those marked as "border-hoppers." In 1992 I sent an inquiry to the Karelian department of the Federal Security Service (the former NKVD-KGB), attaching a ten-page list of names to it. I did receive an answer saying that such identification would take a lot of time, so I'd just have to wait. Wait I did! And, as I realized later, having tackled the problem myself, it was very naive of me to have even considered the possibility of having my question answered: someone had to be specifically assigned to do the job. Alongside with wage-earning it took me almost two years.

9. Names of people occupied in production (KRA).

10. Names of those who had perished in WWII or are still reported missing (KRA).

11. Names of those whose fate is unknown.

12. Papers from Finland's military archives. This was a new source of valuable information: I learned about the fates of numerous Americans and discovered people who, up to that point, had been in the list of "Unknowns."

I was up against the same difficulty as all other researchers: Finnish names are often distorted beyond recognition, so you have to find other papers for verification. Some emigrants bear the same Christian and family name, thus only the birth date, the paternal name, used in all Russian documents, or the passenger list served as a means of defining who the person under consideration really was. But even this essential data was often lacking: in NKVDA papers you could sometimes read, "...has no paternal name." Difficulties were enhanced by the fact that it looked as if in some cases a name had been fixed in Russian by the word of mouth, so you get a very confusing combination of vowels and consonants. Thanks to the availability of several lists identification often appeared possible; but there are names that appear in only one, so it is impossible to vouch for the exact spelling and define who the person we're talking about really is.

I'd like to single out three positive features of my research launched in the summer of 1989. First, the situation was actually such that in Karelia, where Finnish-Americans had for decades worked side by side with locals, no one knew anything about them: who they were, where they had come from. The term Canadians was applied to one and all, it made no difference whether they were from the States or Canada.

Karelian historian A. Andriainen was working on this immigration problem, but his papers didn't reach a large reading public, although they were written in the spirit of the time without any extensive appraisal of the labor and financial contributions the immigrants had made. The fact that it was mentioned at all prevented the spread of his writings. Reading his papers today you find they lack scope and depth in accentuating the vital role Finnish-Americans played in the cultural and economic life of the Republic.[1]

On hearing that so-and-so had come to the Soviet Union from America, Russians living beyond the boundaries of Karelia took it for an error, saying, "Oh, so your parents left for America." It took some explaining to bring home to the listeners that they had come to Russia from America. Nothing, or very, very little was ever said about them in the mass media. So materials appearing in Russian language papers, journals and TV, Moscow TV included, aroused the interest of Russians. Nowadays, when hundreds of thousands have left and are leaving Russia for the United States, Canada, Finland, Sweden, Israel, Germany and other countries the very idea of coming to Russia from the West seems preposterous. You can even hear, "What fools!"

Much more was known about this organized emigration in the West, especially in Finland and America. On the one hand, the emigrants, the "red" Finns were booed by the so-called "white" Finns and, on the other, praised by the radical press for their sincere endeavors to help the first-ever country of workers and peasants get on its feet. The intolerance born between the two groups of Finns in no way promoted research that would have enhanced clarification of the problem.

Profound literature on emigration to the Soviet Union was written and published in the West by such outstanding historians as Reino Kero, Auvo Kostiainen and others, but it was in Finnish or English and never reached the reading public of Russia. Little has been written about the organization of this unheard-of emigration from the West to the East, and I shall touch upon this issue.

Second, people started writing, explaining, trying to bring about reconciliation between the "red" and the "white" Finns. The abyss that had been created due to ideological arguments often tore families apart and it looked as if there could never be any reconciliation. Readers claim that my 1989–90 newspaper articles published in the Petrozavodsk papers, "They Took My Father"[2] and "Red Exodus"[3] can be regarded as a major contribution towards this re-examination of the ill-fated emigration from America. The 1993, N 3 issue of the journal "Carelia" was completely devoted to this problem. It contains revealing articles by Irja Takala, Viktor Paaso, Paula Autio, Ramon Niemi, an interview with Ernest Haapaniemi and other materials. These were in Finnish. The Russian-language journal "Sever" carried Viktor Paaso's lengthy story, the major Russian-language papers "Severny Kuryer" and "Petrozavodsk" have also published numerous articles. It is comprehensible why Petrozavodsk inhabitants keep asking, "When will there be a Russian publication of these materials?" Well, it's on the agenda.

People are writing! The more, the better. There is so much more to be done along these lines that everyone's efforts are to be encouraged.

During my longer stays in the US I had scores of meetings with audiences made up of former "white" Finns. I say "former" because I was happy to hear my listeners say that it was high time to bury the hatchet, that we are all Finns, after all. I've also heard how foolish it was to wage such a war, to disregard the calamities that had become the lot of those who went over. The floodgates opened: Americans began looking for their lost kin. The answers many have received haven't been soothing but…We can pray for the premature loss of innocent souls.

Citizen diplomacy has done a lot to bring about this reconciliation. Duluth's ties with Petrozavodsk and Vermont's relationship with Karelia have been extremely invigorating. What a treat to see people working together, solving issues that have become global. Isn't that what friendship is all about?

Third, getting to the bottom of this mass emigration is important for another reason too. I was prepared for criticism of "Red Exodus" and even wrote that I didn't expect it to be to the liking of one and all. But what happened in reality was depressing. With the publishing of the book a review appeared in the Superior "Työmies" putting the whole story down to Sevander's embitterment over the loss of her father. I lost no time in responding to explain my grounds. My stand was whole-heartedly supported by Harry Siitonen but that's where the discussion stopped. Why? Wasn't this another manifestation of intolerance, intolerance to criticism aimed at unmasking the failure of the insane experiment to install socialism by force? I would have enjoyed a serious debate that might have brought some hard-liners and doubting folk round to a new way of thinking. But no! The paper had been taken over by a new editor, who just nipped the debate in the bud. We, those who had gone to Russia, once again appeared in the line of defectors trying to paint innocent Russia and Stalin black. Such an understanding of the 70 years of Russian history is dangerous!

The ultimate aim of my efforts is not to preach socialism or decry capitalism. I'll leave that to politicians, sociologists, and economists: they have the tools, experience and knowledge. But I do hope that my efforts, based on experience, show that socialism should not be identified with Lenin and Stalin. The essence of their leadership was based on POWER, the power for a minority to rule a majority at any cost. Their "socialism" "thrived" on forced labor, on millions of victims. Their "socialism" caught innocent non-suspecting masses, including thousands of foreigners, Finnish-Americans among them, in the swift current that theoretically was to bring them to a happy future, but in reality led them to disaster.

Openness in Russia gave rise to a flood of publications exposing the ruling Communist party's policy. Some titles suffice to understand what the papers are about, i.e. parliamentarian Stanislav Govorukhin's pamphlet "The Great Criminal Revolution" (1917), Bunich's "The Party's Gold. An historical chronicle." But I'd strongly recommend those who still have doubts as to the personalities of the Soviet "fuhrers" to take up the recent substantial works of Russian historians and philosophers Dmitrii Volkogonov[4] and Edward Radzinsky.[5] Another useful author in this respect would be Arkadi Vaxberg, who unmasks the formerly all-mighty Comintern, depicting this policy in its true colors.[6]

After all the changes that have occurred and are taking place in Western and Eastern Europe, one's understanding of the –isms today shouldn't be primitive. The danger of betting on the wrong horse is always there."Ghosts from the past will re-enter the stage in new disguise," that's how Daniel Singer sums it up expertly.[7] Neo-fascists in Germany (and Russia!!!), Le Pen in France, "skinheads" in Scandinavia, Zhirinovsky and extreme left-wing communist Viktor Anpilov in Russia are enough to put us on the alert.

Russia! The country where I've spent most of my life, is now in a state of turmoil. With family, colleagues, dearest friends, hundreds of former students among them, I can't remain indifferent to its fate. I'm writing this long before the June 1996, presidential elections. Their outcome, regardless of the frenzied efforts of pro-Yeltsin circles, might be in favor of communist Zyuganov and his party. Why do I think so?

The challenge of democracy was appealing and it was accepted. Accepted, but not fought for by the Establishment. Yes, there was a fight but not for what democracy is all about. It turned into a fight for wealth: who could grow richer and quicker? The people lost their savings; (for many it was no more than the so-called funereal money). Some welfare benefits disappeared. Sky-rocketing inflation makes sheer existence a problem. The most hard-hit part of the population turned out to be the seniors, those who had created the national wealth, and... children! When I returned to Russia in 1993 after a year-long absence, what struck me most in the street scene was the almost complete absence of expectant mothers and mothers, fathers or grannies out for a walk with a baby buggy. The death rate is growing and the birth rate is dropping. There are places in Russia where they are equal or, even worse, the former takes the lead.

Nostalgia for the formerly low, as compared to the West, living standards was what brought the communists in on a white horse in the December 1995 elections. Nostalgia for the secure past, consequently for the communist regime, is the trump the communist party is playing. The man-in-the-street is not aware of the fact, that Zyuganov, like all other present-day leaders, who seemingly come out as partisans of state-owned (what the nostalgic masses attach importance to) property, are in reality already owners of this property belonging to them in shares. What we witness today is the capitalist-turned functionaries who want to run the country in the same way as when they were party bosses, but on a wealthier economic basis. It is not for nothing that Zyuganov claims the communists of today are not the communists of the past. There's no denying the truthfulness of this statement. Only what the voter doesn't seem to notice is the same erroneous identification of Zyuganov with the interests of the nation.

The rising popularity of Zyuganov and party has introduced another dangerous phenomenon: the disbelief of some sections of the population in the outrages committed by the Leninist-Stalinist regimes. Why not try all over again?

Even if Yeltsin should come out on the top, it would mean having a president elected on the least evil principle. A sad choice! A sad choice with unpredictable consequences for a great country like Russia that's on serious crossroads of history.

I couldn't refrain from expressing these thoughts that stem from experience, observations and studies, thoughts that express my deep concern for the fates of people I love.

1 Going or not going?

That was the question being asked by many US and Canadian communists and socialist-minded people. Answering it was not easy. Moving is always a problem: from house to house, from apartment to apartment, from town to town! But from country to country? From a developed civilized country to a backward one, one which very little is even known about? Judging by history, Finns have moving in their blood! And when there are no major moves to be made, they begin changing the furniture around. At least that's what happened to Mother when we came to Petrozavodsk. Every other Saturday on coming home from school we saw that Mother had been "moving" again!

I was surprised to discover KRA papers that throw light upon the twenties when activities promoting assistance to Russia were already under way. As early as in 1920, a Russian Relief Committee was organized by the Finnish Association of the Socialist party in Duluth. They appeared in other places too. The 1920–29 activities of this group in Duluth are frugally reflected in KRA protocols. By the way, at the time Gus Hall, who later became Secretary General of the American Communist party, was manager of the Association.

Going through these papers was exciting for me: I stumbled into many familiar names: Puro, Halonen, Mattson, Tenhunen, etc, and even that of Swiss-born Finnish-American Lillian Lehtimäki, whose singing had won over audiences in many countries. The proceeds of the concert she gave on May 9, 1924 at the Superior Hall were donated to this fund.

The KRA have also preserved some protocols of meetings held by the Finnish Association of the Socialist party in Worcester, Mass.(1921–26). The Duluth and Worcester socialists raised numerous questions directly or indirectly pertaining to the issue under consideration: moving "Työmies" to the Midwest, creating a Workers' party center, collecting money for the "Kuzbas fund," fund-raising affairs to help Russia, rendering assistance to a Chisholm, Minn., family that had lost its breadwinner: he was picked up for spreading "Soviet Russia."

There was counter-action too. In a letter from Leo Leino (Petrozavodsk) to the Heikkinens living in Moscow, the author describes the activities of Aino Morton in New York. He claimed that "she was interfering with organizing the emigration of people to Karelia." Leino explains, that "in inviting people to come to Russia we are supported by a revolutionary right, by the right to build socialism in this country. We enjoy the right to accept non-party members, supportive of the ideals of the proletariat, from America." A. Morton's letters sent out to perspective emigrants from America are signed "Secretary of the Finnish Offices." "Evidently the writer," Leino claims, "is a young American woman to whom matters have been explained upside-down. It's regretful to see on what level an influential person, who accuses Leino, stands. She makes a mess of things and causes confusion by writing to workers that it is she who can arrange their trip to Karelia."

It looks as if Leino had no idea of who Aino Morton really was: a person close to Kremlin circles and Otto Kuusinen's wife. Upon reading Aino Kuusinen's "Jumala Syöksee Enkelinsä", the name Aino Morton set a bell ringing. Interesting to note that in 1973 the original was smuggled into Russia by a friend of mine. It was translated into Russian, abridged, 15 years later. Slow but sure times were changing!

Up to 1989 I had a reliable consultant on problems connected with the American workers' movement—my father-in-law Kuuno Sevander. I talked with him about Aino Morton and he asked whether our family hadn't met with a person bearing that name during our New York period of life. These words helped to recreate the vision of a beautiful, well-groomed lady and a heated argument she was having with Father during her visit. I didn't know what the discussion was all about, but now I can presume that she was less idealistic and more realistic, when it came to Kremlin moves, than my dad, and that probably she was trying to talk him out of the whole escapade. But no! He was "guilty" of having talked people into going over and that's where we were headed for ourselves by the time!

The radical papers "Työmies," "Eteenpäin," "Raivaaja," "Toveri," "Vapaus" were published in the states where the enclaves of Finns were the largest, and this media kept fanning the interest of their readers in the emigration project. It is not for nothing that in the United States the highest number of emigrants from the US came from Michigan, Minnesota, New York, Massachusetts, Wisconsin, Illinois, Washington and Oregon. Ohio, too, gave a high number of future Karelians, as activities of the "red" Finns there were high.

When it comes to defining the number of emigrants from Canada, it's much more difficult for the following reasons: first, only personal contacts with those who wrote or met with me in 1989–90 gave exact data on their home localities; second, many Canadians were single; they numbered highest among the loggers who came to Karelia to get the forestry industry started. Where did I get their names? Sad to admit, but they come from the NKVDA which gave only one line of information: arrived from Canada in

Actors and singers at the Fitchburg, Mass. Hall. Circa 1929. First row, second from left: Mrs. Leini. Courtesy of Leini Marie.

1931 (...1932, 1933, 1934). Quite often the year wasn't indicated at all. Still, it's worthwhile singling out such Canadian localities as Cobalt, Vancouver, Rosegrove, Sudbury, Webster's Corner, St. Sault Marie, Ontario and Port William (Thunder Bay). Thus the number of emigrants from Canada has increased largely as compared to the figures given in "Red Exodus."

The seed for emigration to Russia was planted as early as in 1921–23. The early settlers from America who had chosen the warm parts of a south-Russian region—Rostov, or the fishermen and families who had settled down on the cold forbidding White Sea coast, or the enthusiastic builders of the industrial giant Magnitogorsk, that was going up in the Urals, were enthusiasts. They kept those back home well-informed of their endeavors which seemed promising at the start. The news had a favorable impact in America. In fact there even were families who returned to America but went back to Russia (the Johan and Maria Kaipainens from Buffalo, N.Y., the Arthur and Aino Ketola family from Calgary, Canada, the Lauri and Lyyli Rautanen family from Ontaganon, Mich., the Yrjö and Anna Laine family from Scranton, Penn. and a few more). Naturally the returnees included the rightfully disillusioned too. They returned and remained in America, but a sense of political commitment withheld some from criticism. Still it's not easy to understand what kept them in the ranks of staunch defenders of socialism after the grave disappointment they had experienced in Russia. Others, after getting their fill of "socialism", gave up their party activities, moved to other localities and became normal, apolitical citizens.

As early as in 1922 Matti Tenhunen visited Russia at the invitation of Karelian leaders Gylling and Rovio to conduct talks on the possibility of getting Finnish-Americans interested in coming to Russia to build socialism. There was no consensus on this issue as yet. The idea didn't find support in the Kremlin, nor did it get the support of the American communist party, although the Canadian Communist party's stand was positive. Stalin and Molotov agreed to Karelia's renewed proposals only when it became obvious to the Russian leaders that there was no way to get the Karelian economy going without foreign help: the country's need for quality timber was acute!

That's when recruiting actually began and at a quick pace at that. But we must bear in mind that there were circumstances which alleviated the recruiting. First, the advocates of the Cause were not plowing virgin land: Russia had already been in the picture for over ten years. Second, the international proletarian inclinations of the Finnish-American working-class left no doubt. Third, the Great Depression came knocking at the door. People in large industrial centers, e.g. Detroit, were most hard-hit.

Tenhunen's response to the Russian leaders' re-examination of their positions on the immigration problem came without delay. In an article for American readers "Neuvosto-Karjalan kysymyksiä" (Karjalan Teknillisen Avun Lehtinen N 4,1930) he came out with some specific advice (the dating does not seem in accordance, but we already know that recruiting was going on before the KTA took shape!):

The wrong notion: I've got to get going because there's no way to get along here any more.

The right notion: I've got to get going to help train the local labor force; I can't be a burden to Karelia; the most important professions are: loggers, farmers, steel workers, printers, quarry specialists. I've got to pay my own passage to Leningrad, a little help may be found, but not to turn to the KTA.

Buying machines and tools. Don't buy in inland stores. Use Amtorg checks (the Amtorg was a trade organization in New York with which the Soviet Union maintained contacts). Receipts from Amtorg entitle the purchaser to be refunded in Russia. It has been agreed upon that each traveller buys machines and tools which he himself needs in his profession. But the impossibility to purchase machines and equipment should not serve as an impediment in getting American labor force over to Russia. Besides an increase in organized emigration from America Tenhunen's letter had another unexpected repercussion. A group of 50 American tourists visiting Moscow had hunted up Tenhunen requesting to be employed on a contract basis as they were willing to stay and help. There's no evidence to prove whether this worked or not.

The emigration requirements were elaborated on the Soviet side: the necessity to get foreign workers ideologically devoted to the cause of socialism; to ensure that these immigrants would arrive not only with their know-how, but that they'd bring along the badly needed tools and instruments to work with; the basis for a "machine fund" in foreign currency was to be laid with their help.(See KTA paper reproduced at the end of this chapter. Two paragraphs have a translation). Each traveller was allowed to bring equipment into the country customs-free; local authorities were granted the right to sell a possible excess of goods to other parts of the country at a higher price; the crossing of immigrants was to be made at their own expense. The Soviets guaranteed the refunding of all expenses in gold rubles i.e. 2 rbls for

$1. (at such a currency exchange rate the scales tipped heavily in favor of Russia).

Heaps of work born in connection with the influx of foreigners from the US, Canada and Finland, made it necessary to create a special organ, whose duty it would be to make all the arrangements connected with immigration. Thus on October 9, 1931, the Karelian Council of People's Commissariats (KCPC) adopted the decision to establish The Resettling Management, which began its activities on October 15 the same year. Soon Matti Tenhunen appeared on the Petrozavodsk scene. At the recommendation of Gylling, he was appointed Head of the Labor department of KCPC. Problems connected with immigration kept cropping up. Among those Tenhunen had to solve were urgent ones: providing the arrivals with accommodation, immediate jobs, establishing higher production quotas for foreigners, supplying them with better food than was available for the local population. In major Russian cities, where foreigners were under contract, the requirement for better provisions had already brought into being the "Insnab" (Provisions for Foreigners. Deficient goods were sold at the usual average prices, only the quantity was limited) and the "Torgsin." The "Torgsin" stores sold goods only in exchange for hard currency or valuables. (Nowadays with the restructuring of economy in Russia time and again these "Insnab" and "Torgsin" stores come to mind. Why? When you see how many go to the shops like to a museum /forbidding prices!/ you're overwhelmed with a sense of shame: you see almost anything your heart could desire, but... Such privileges that foreigners enjoyed up to 1935 couldn't breed fraternal feelings in those who didn't!).

The 1931 plan alone provided for recruiting 2,000 loggers to Karelia! An active correspondence was being carried on between Petrozavodsk, on the one hand, and New York, Washington, Chicago and Ontario, on the other. Karelia was displaying active interest in speeding up the organizational work in America.

American and Canadian communist party members best endowed with speakers' talents, a knowledge of Russia and the political situation started their rounds, meeting with people at local halls or at homes, where coffee and "pulla" was always generously served. Only today has it become possible to judge the extremely inadequate, insufficient knowledge of the domestic political scene in Russia, that those people had. It's paradoxical that recruiting to Russia was triggered off in America at a time when the antipopular phenomenon of "special resettling of national minorities" from their historical lands to far-away Siberia, the north with its permafrost and the Far East was in full swing in Russia.[8] Only a few years would pass before the Ingrian Finnish population, inhabiting villages surrounding Leningrad, was to meet with the same tragic fate. War was looming on the horizon. The Russian regime knew how to hide its secrets!

Juxtaposed with the gloom and tragedy of the-then Russia that I'm NOW aware of, I recalled one of the "recruiting" trips I made with my father. In the early spring of 1996 driving through Floodwood, Minnesota, with a friend I related an incident that had occurred in this little town when I was knee-high to a grasshopper. On a beautiful cloudless summer day I begged Dad to let me go along on his speaking trip. He did and it wasn't the first time either. When we got to Floodwood, it was nap time and Father had to get a haircut before he gave his talk, so I was left with the lady of the house. On waking my first question was, "Where's Daddy?" "Oh," she said, "we have no little girl, so he left you to us. You're going to like it here, that's for sure." I only remember shutting up like a clam, stealing down the staircase, going out and setting off on foot along the road we had come. When Dad came and didn't find me, the episode was related. Knowing what I'd do under the circumstances, Father got the car going and drove off in search of me. I must have walked quite a distance and grown tired in the heat, because he found me sleeping in the shade of a tree by the roadside.

The fertile soil the recruiters were tilling started bearing fruit: in 1930 applications to Karelian authorities were pouring in. Letters came connected not only with emigration requests but also with offers for technological and spiritual help. S. Wirta from Eureka, California, wrote about a one-man-electricity-or-gas-run saw he had designed. He intended to send it over with a Pesola to train loggers in using it, as he himself wasn't planning to make the crossing. Wirta stressed the advantages of the saw: weight 130 pounds (the old one weighed 225 lb). Emil Rautanen, Iron River, Mich., donated $1000 worth of machinery from his metal shop to be sent to Karelia. Inspired by the events in Russia Antti Wiitanen from Gardner, Mass., had composed some revolutionary music and L. Laukkanen was writing a play.

To cope with the organization of affairs, to make them run smoothly, agencies of the Karelian Technical Aid were created in New York and Toronto. The New York agency launched its activities on May 1, 1931 with M.Tenhunen at the head. Soon Tenhunen was replaced by Kalle Aronen

(Brooklyn, New York) and in March, 1932 by Oscar Corgan, who worked in that capacity until the KTA was closed down and on April 2, 1934 that family, too, took off for Karelia. Mr. Latva headed the Canadian Technical Aid agency from the start up to the end.

Applications of those who expressed the desire to leave were not accepted at random. It was quite a procedure. Communist party members were to have the official permission of their Central Committee. From June 1931 to March 1932, 71 American communist party members were granted this permission. But many were refused, as it was not in the best interests of the party to lose its activists. As a rule they complained, insisting on their right to go to Russia with their comrades. But they received letters of the following kind, "Aug.1, 1931, to Alex Viita. Our instructions are to stick to the rule of not accepting applications from Party members that have not received permission to travel. We can't and don't intend to break these rules. Thus we consider your case closed. Comradely greetings. Kalle Aronen." Similar refusals were sent to Theodore Sauso, Matti Lakkila, and John Oravainen from Astoria, Oregon. Their situation differed greatly from that of their peers: They were under threat of deportation due to their political activities. Probably that is why their request for permission to leave was granted and they found themselves in Karelia by the end of 1931.

The emigration project was worked out in Russia and it called for 2850 lumber workers, carpenters, sawmill operators, tractor drivers, auto and tractor mechanics, granite workers, machine operators. Out of the total number of loggers 1000 were to come from Canada.

This is how the system worked:

First, the applicants filled in forms, attached three passport photos and a doctor's certificate to it.

Second, these papers went to a general meeting of a local Finnish Federation. Here a decision was passed on the applicant's political and trade abilities. If satisfactory, they were signed and sealed by the presiding officers and sent on to the KTA offices.

Third, a committee of three, two from the Finnish bureau and one from the KTA, after a final examination and approval of the papers, forwarded them to Narkomtrud (Labor Commissariat) in Petrozavodsk. This was the final stage of the visa application. Archive papers show that by July 17, 1931, 683 applications (242 of them from women) had already been forwarded and visas had been issued for 186 applicants; 22 of them had already sailed.

A few words about the second stage. Protocols illustrate what a serious stand was taken by members of the Finnish Federation, how they really tried to live up to the requirement of sending the right sort of people to the Soviet Union. Discussions of perspective candidates were heated. Sometimes they ended with refusals. The main grounds on which a party was refused: addiction to alcohol, womanizing, passivity in social work, a refusal to subscribe for the socialist papers, negligence in reading the workers' press, etc. A Sept.14, 1931 protocol from Rock, Mich., shows that Mrs. Davidson got only a scarce majority of votes. Those who participated in the discussion based their doubts on the fact that she hadn't sold her property. Didn't it look as if she harbored plans of returning to America? She made no bones of it, saying that she was going because her husband was all for it, but if she made up her mind to leave, leave she would, even if her husband decided to stay. Unfortunately Hilda wasn't fated to live a happy life: she met with a mortal accident in 1933 and her idealist husband Jack stayed behind only to be picked up by NKVD agents and executed. An extensive exchange of correspondence between Frank Niinivaara from Enfield, New Hampshire and the Federation took place before his papers were finalized. Otto Granholm's complaint went straight to Leino in Petrozavodsk and he was accepted. Both men's persistence got the same reward: execution!

It happened that sometimes remonstrance on the spot didn't satisfy the applicant, so the local Federation turned to the KTA. Such a complaint came from Fort Bragg, California. "C.H. is so intent on going to Karelia that he wants to leave his elderly wife behind with their daughter. But it's really his son-in-law who got him all keyed-up". Here's what C.H. writes in his application, "Hän on korjannut lissuni ja ostanut taijerit, joten matkavaakani alkaa olla reilassa New Yorkin matkaa varten". This situation must have had a happy ending since neither father nor son-in-law showed up in Karelia.

Not always were the negative resolutions adopted by branches of the Federation justifiable. For example the one concerning Hjalmar (Joonas) Harju from Ilwaco, Washington. His perseverance got him to Karelia, where he made a huge material contribution to the development of agriculture in Karelia. Refusals, signed by Aronen, were also sent out to Oscar Freeman, Mauri and Hilma Heino, Toivo, Hilda and Edith Lehtinen, Jorgen and Helen Lund, Walter Mäki, Aldrick Sandelin. But if at once you don't succeed, try, try, try again! And so they did. A Finn wouldn't be a

Finn without principality and perseverance. He's sure to go out of his way to prove his righteousness if undeservedly daunted. (Ne itsepäiset suomalaiset!) It was this quality that paved the way to Russia for many a family, which, beyond doubt, would have been happy back Home. But the contribution of each of the above-mentioned persons to the national economy of Karelia was praiseworthy! When I told Edie Lehtinen about this finding, all she could say was, "Was there ever another so idealistic and persevering a species as the crazy Finnish-Americans that left for Russia? I realize what our life in Grand Rapids would have been like if my parents had accepted that first refusal." Edith, my cherished friend of the stormy thirties and from thereon, joined her parents in the ever after on March 1, 1996. So, probably we should regard some of the refusals that come our way from time to time as a blessing?

All in all 265 adults, 179 men and 86 women inclusively, who had addressed the KTA, were refused visas.

A brief comparison of visa applications and passenger lists shows that many would-be emigrants changed their mind and did not end up on Karelian or other Russian soil. In the KRA there's one paper to this effect dated November 14, 1933. "The number of visas granted to would-be emigrants from the US and Canada, but not used is:

men	women	children	Total
1581	678	292	2552."

This figure is high and it speaks volumes! The sharp decrease in emigration from America in 1932 is vital proof of the fact that some Finnish Americans were coming to their senses, that their decision-making was much more mature than that of the first thousands who had taken the leap. How they must have rejoiced in not making the fatal error that was so perilous for friends and relatives. Relatives! That's an issue! How many times I've heard from my peers, "We came only because we learned that uncle's/aunt's family was going. If only we had stayed where we belonged. If only..." But blood is thicker than water! Many have visited the homeland they left behind, seen its beauty and prosperity, experienced the benefits of its social climate; others haven't. But, on seeing postcards of San Francisco, Duluth, Boston, Seattle, Minneapolis, Vancouver, Thunder Bay..., what can they do but heave a deep sigh? The road to the US and Canada is open for those who are citizens by birth but very few of us have taken advantage of this generous opportunity. A much greater number have chosen Finland, the land of their forefathers. That's where they have decided to spend the sunset of their lives.

I've listened to many sad stories of parting told by my peers. The better-off the family, the harder it was to leave! The warmer and more emotional the send-off of comrades, the more cherished the memories. And every family or group of families embarking on this road to the Unknown was truly seen off in good style. Probably those who were remaining behind looked upon us thinking, "What on earth are they up to? Do they truly believe in finding what they are looking for—secure jobs and living conditions, a Finnish language environment, a guaranteed future for their children, the possibility of creating a land where every working man could prosper, benefit himself and the nation…?"

Many a time have my brother Paul, sister Aino and I recollected the warmth of the farewell party given to our family in the theater hall of the Työn Temppeli on 126th Street, New York on the eve of our departure. Over 400 well-wishers had come to bid us good-bye. Among the wonderful things in the Hall that we were leaving behind was the sauna with its swimming pool, the cafeteria and one little thing I prided myself on: the one and only sports trophy I've ever won: a statuette with four names on it, including Mayme Ahti and Mayme Corgan. Holding it in my hands for the last time, I wondered whether I'd ever see Billy (to avoid confusion I was Bobby) again. The next day a cheering crowd was at the pier to see us off on board the Kungsholm, waving good-byes.

Our third class cabins were packed with gifts, among them a fur coat our neighbor, Mrs. Milda Vuorela, had gotten from her millionaire mistress and decided would probably come in handy in the cold climate on the other side of the ocean. She had a special liking for Paul and his gifts from her were numerous.

We were very down-to-earth people and never talked about premonitions or omens. But looking back on the late afternoon of April 4, 1934, we could have got a hunch. The bright sun was setting into clouds, a wind was gaining momentum, a storm was on the point of breaking out. And it did. Bad weather accompanied us all the way to Göteborg. These signs of nature could've been deciphered as, "Watch your step"! Nothing of the kind! We were a happy resolute family, off to join friends and looking forward to a reunion with Mom's sister Mari's family the Nissinens, who had left the States for Finland and were to join us in Karelia. Didn't that make Mother happy!

Our family was on its own. But how many groups we had seen off in New York! Each of them left behind highly charged ideological farewell messages, an orchestra played the "International," hundreds were singing in Finnish or English, "Arise, ye prisoners of starvation!"

Decisions made, passports with visas obtained, property sold, belongings packed, including warm clothing bought for the rightfully expected rigid climate, money transferred to Amtorg, all the good-byes, many of which were irreversible, said. Ready! Set! Go!

Circulating letter N 1-33.

ADVICE TO THOSE DEPARTING FOR SOVIET KARELIA
(Translation of the third and fourth paragraphs).

We bear responsibility only for donations to the MACHINE FUND. On the basis of a KTA receipt you are entitled to be reimbursed in keeping with the Soviet exchange rate. The Karelian Resettling Management is responsible for this reimbursement.

When you come to the USSR border, declare all your money to the customs officials. They will confirm your currency and there's no danger of anybody taking it away from you. Vice versa it will help you later if you intend to make a visit abroad: the receipt will enable you to carry your money across the border. At present in the Soviet Union and in Karelia too you can buy goods in the foreign currency stores which are probably not available in rubles. Thus foreign currency can be used advantageously within Soviet borders too. Beware of exchanging foreign currency with anyone else as it is strictly forbidden. When the need to exchange currency arises, turn to the State bank. Selling goods to private persons is also forbidden: you have been granted customs-free entrance as you are bringing in goods only for YOUR OWN PERSONAL needs.

Comradely greetings,

The S. Karelian Technical Aid

Kiertokirje No.1 -33

Ohjeita Neuvosto-Karjalaan meneville.

Neuvosto-Karjalan Siirtolaishallinnolta saatujen ohjeiden mukaisesti emme voi tälläkertaa lähettää Karjalaan kaikkia niitä joilla on olemassa matkalupa, vaan täytyy jokaisen matkasta sopia kanssamme etukäteen. Matkalle lähtön jokaiselle määrittelemme ammatin perusteella, sillä vaan vissejä ammattilaisia voidaan lähettää. Tiedottakaa meille matkaaikeistanne ja vasta luvan saatuanne alatte valmistautua lähtöä varten. Kirjeessä tiedotamme teille sitten matka-ajan sekä mitä tietä matkanne tulee tapahtumaan. Kun tietotatte halustanne matkustaa, niin antakaa tietää ammattinne ja myös lisä ammatit mihin kykenette.

Siirtolaishallinnon toivomuksen mukaisesti selostamme uudelleen että jokainen voi lainata persoonakohtaisesti matkarahaa tovereilleen, kuitenkin siinä selvässä ymmärryksessä, että siirtolaishallinto eikä Karjalan Teknillinen Apu ole näistä lainoista millään tavalla edesvastuussa, vaan itse huollatte niiden perimisestä.

Ainoastaan KONERAHASTOON luovutetuista varoista olemme edesvastuussa, joista Karjalan Teknillisen Avun antamalla kuitilla saatte periä rahanne takaisin Neuvostomaan rahassa vallitsevan kurssin mukaan. Konerahojen takaisin maksusta huoltaa Karjalan Siirtolaishallinto.

Kun saavutte Neuvostoliiton rajalle, niin rekisteratkaa kaikki rahanne tullivirkailijoille. Ne antaa teille kuitin rahoistanne eikä ole mitään pelkoa, että ne niitä teiltä pois ottaisi. Päinvastoin se auttaa teitä siinä suhteessa jos myöhemmällä tulisi tarpeelliseksi käydä rajan toisella puolella, niin saamanne rekisteraus kuitti oikeuttaa teidät kulettamaan valuuttaa mukananne. Nykyisin voi Neuvostoliitossa ja samoin Karjalassa ulkomaanrahalla ostaa valuutta kaupoista sellaisia tarvikkeita joita mahdollisesti ei saa ruplilla ostettua. Siis ulkomaan rahaa voi edullisesti käyttää Neuvostoliiton rajojen sisällä. Varokaa myöskin vaihtamasta ulkomaanrahaa rupliin kenenkään kanssa sillä sellainen on jyrkästi kielletty. Silloin kun tulee tarpeelliseksi vaihtaa, tulee sen suorittaa valtion pankkilaitoksen välityksellä. Samoin kaikenlaisten tavaroiden myynti yksityisille on kielletty, sen takia, että tullivapauden tavaroillenne saatte sillä perusteella, että viette ne OMAA KÄYTTÖÄNNE varten.

Matkatavaroiden järjestämisessä pitää ennen annetut ohjeet paikkansa. Laatikot eivät saisi painaa yli 250 paunaa. Ne tulee olla vahvoja ja hyvästi naulatut, sekä joko köytetty tai rautavanteella ympäröity. Kun on useampia laatikoita, numeroikaa laatikkonne ja pankaa taskukirjaanne ylös mitä kussakin laatikossa on. Kaikkien koneiden numerot myös pankaa huolellisesti muistiin, ja hyvä on sekin, että merkitsee laatikon päälle, koneen nimen ja numeron. Kaikki asioiden näin järjestely auttaa teitä Neuvostoliiton tullitarkastuksessa ja säästytte monen laatikon avaamiselta jos tarkalleen näin menettelette. Rifla pyssyjä ja taskuaseita ei saa viedä, ainoastaan 22 kaliperin ja haulipyssyn, vaan nekin pitää tullissa ilmoittaa. Yksinäiset miehet eivät voi viedä naisten tavaroita, eikä naiset miesten. Perheen mukana taas voi viedä molempia. Jos toiselle vie tavaraa, täytyy viedä omanaan. Paperilappu osoitteet usein lähtevät irti ja niin laatikot joutuvat sattumalta väärille teille. Siksi onkin paras kirjoittaa laatikon laitaan, ainaskin kahdelle sivulle mustalla maalilla täysi nimenne sekä osoite: PETROZAVODSK via LENINGRAD, U.S.S.R.

Toverit, näitä ohjeita on tarkoin seurattava valmistautuessanne matkalle Neuvosto Karjalaan.

Toveruudella,

N. KARJALAN TEKNILLINEN APU

K:tta

2 Going

On board the S.S. Kungsholm, April 6, 1934. Katri, Aino and Oscar Corgan. From the Corgans' archive.

Crossing the ocean nowadays is quite a different sensation as compared with the past. I've lost count of my numerous flights above the Atlantic and once above the Pacific. You see next to nothing. You learn nothing, unless an exceptionally good film is running, like "Dead Poets' Society," which I had the luck to see once. Even a 15-hour non-stop flight doesn't contribute much to striking up lasting acquaintances, to challenging beliefs, maybe even to changing them. Making a sea voyage, lasting for 7–9 days, especially if different kinds of activities are going on is quite another thing. Often lasting friendships are tied and there are romances that lead to matrimony.

It might be that the crossings the Finnish-Americans made in the early thirties either confirmed them in their socialist convictions or shook the beliefs of a few. It could have spelled confirmation for "the true proletarian cadres," disillusion for the "fellow-travellers" and final decision-making for the group that was in-between.[9] And why?

There is a Russian-born term "zaorganizovannost," meaning "over-organized." An excess of orderliness always leaves a bad taste in the mouth, as it implies a lack of initiative, a system of command. By the way, the very existence of the Russian regime depended on this non-democratic system of enforcing action and decision-making upon its citizens. It was sickening.

Working with RKA materials I was once again, after my earlier acquaintance with American communist press articles, unfavorably impressed by the strong similarity between the style of the language used in Russia and that of American communists. This language allowed no objections. It can be traced in the American communist press, in protocols of meetings, in the farewell messages of scores of groups headed for Russia. What is the root of this similarity? Intolerance! Intolerance with anything that runs counter to ideas expounded by communist philosophy. This is how things should be done and in no other way! This was manifested during the crossings the Finnish-Americans made, too.

What the KTA excelled in was the organization of groups getting across to Russia. The main carrier was the Swedish-American Line (SAL) amplified by other carriers when the number of passengers increased beyond the possibilities of the SAL. This transportation system was working so efficiently that on Oct.13, 1931, Tenhunen received a letter from the SAL offering to expand its operations in 1932 up to 8,000–10,000 passengers. Another enticing feature of this offer was to arrange direct transportation from New York to Leningrad. A direct trip would require 400 Leningrad-bound passengers per sailing. Why this never occurred can be explained by the fact that the number of passengers began decreasing already in an early stage of the emigration, thus a further drop was predictable for sober-minded analysts. As you know, the KTA in New York and Toronto had just been established in May 1931. June 1931 saw the peak of the emigration: 544 departees from the USA, 596 from Canada. Never again would the monthly figure of emigration exceed 1140.

The fact that contracts with the SAL provided for a number of free-of-charge passages cannot be overlooked. Decisions as to who should benefit by this were made at the KTA meetings. I discovered only one paper to this effect in the KRA papers, although we may presume that there were others as well. In the period from August 1, 1931 to March 24, 1932, that is within eight months of sea travels, 37 future Karelians out of 1068 leaving the USA made the passage free of charge. Unemployment in America had put many men on the dole and the Chosen might have thought they were getting a break, that Karelia would provide them with a golden opportunity. Undoubtedly they were happy boarding their ships. Not knowing their names I can't say who the "lucky" ones were. Who knows, it might have turned out that this was their passage to hell and not to the envisaged stability they had in mind.

As the move was a serious one many families decided it would be better for the bread-winner to go first to see how the land lies. Since a number of those men appear on the returnee lists, it's evident that a wise decision was made: not to reunite with the family on Russian territory but back home in America. Nevertheless the number of wives who followed their husbands either alone or with children is high. In many cases it was quite difficult to make out who this or that wife actually belonged to, especially while dealing with a Mäki, a Kangas, a Salo or other typically Finnish names the lists abound in. An interesting detail. In the first years of Karelian life quite a few Finnish-American ladies paid visits to relatives in Finland. Many returned but many didn't. This time the women-folk took the initiative and went scouting the possibilities of returning. The men followed. This was quite natural as it's always the wife and mother of a family that bears the brunt of difficulties and, on seeing what they were actually up against, it didn't take them long to make up their minds.

The New York KTA cooperated closely with the Canadian KTA. Thus the route in all cases but two on the SAL was New York–Halifax. The ships carried their passengers to the ports of Göteborg or Stockholm, in a few cases to Helsinki. There they boarded smaller ships, usually the Kastelholm, to Leningrad. Two groups went to Revel (Tallinn) and from there on to Leningrad.

Although the Karelia-bound passengers had purchased a huge amount of goods in America, their fancy was caught by Swedish hardware and bicycles. So new goods were bought and taken on board. Mauno Maunumaki alone from Kirkland Lake, Canada, picked up several boxes of nails, as he had heard that they were in short supply over there and he was bent on construction.

On one of the crossings a sad event occurred: teenager Lempi Telin had fallen seriously ill. Since no improvement in her case was observed she was taken to a Göteborg hospital where she unfortunately passed away. In one of the protocols we read, "The funeral of the young girl from a working-class family turned into a modest manifestation of the poor." A highly political assessment of grief, don't you think so? I don't know whether Fanni Telin died of grief in Kondopoga, where the bereaved parents lived and worked. Kustaa Telin, the father, was among the numerous Finns arrested from Kondopoga and executed.

Upon leaving New York harbor a steering committee began preparations for the voyage. After taking on the Canadians, election meetings were held to hand out the "ministerial" posts which, as a rule, were divided 50-50 among US and Canadian departees. Every group had a chairman, a secretary and a board of ten. In addition, a correspondent was elected, a cultural committee, an organizational committee, which also included a children's committee if there was a number of underaged on board. The correspondent was to maintain contact with the KTA and, with the help of passengers, issue bulletins and wall newspapers reflecting activities of the group on board. There were cases when someone violated the anti-alcoholic rules and he was quick to find himself a topic of ridicule.

Every group held from six to nine meetings and they took minutes. Meetings seemed to be popular with the Finns. I remember the evenings at home in the States when we kids were often left to our own devices while both parents were at current meetings. On shipboard the situation was quite the same. The only difference was that the kids were kept in narrow confinements—those of the ship. There was no danger of their getting lost. Besides, the children's committee attempted to arrange their leisure when the grown-ups were busy.

It doesn't pay to quote many protocols: they bear a strong resemblance. I'll limit myself to two just to give the reader an idea of the steadfast ideology. They reflect the way some passengers' minds ran.

Niilo W., secretary of a Kungsholm group that sailed out of New York harbor, composed a cable intended for publication in the "Eteenpäin." "We, about 100 US and Canadian workers, express our protest against racism and the planned murder of the Scottsboro youths. We demand their immediate release. Down with capitalist exploitation! Down with capitalist wars! Long live the Soviet Union and the World Revolution!"

The final protocol of group N 23, dated July 1, 1932, was written on the last lap of its journey on board the "Kastelholm." "Expressing the opinion of our group about information based on news received from the Soviet Union and Karelia, which mainly touches upon difficulties, obstacles and deficiencies in Karelia, to where we are bound, we express our readiness to accept the obligations, set before us by the Karelian and Soviet governments; we unanimously promise to subject ourselves to decisions adopted by central organs, as well as those of elected bodies which in future may be adopted. In practical constructional labor devoted to the development of the Soviet Union, we pledge to do our best, regardless of conditions. We promise to subject our comrades who do not conform to unanimously adopted decisions to a Comrades' court discussion; in cases where a violation of rules is more serious, we pledge to have higher standing organs discuss the behavior of such a person. We promise to behave in a comradely fashion with one another in work and leisure, in discussions, to practice self-criticism, to subjugate ourselves to the will of the majority. We promise to fight for the Soviet

Union and for the exploited working class of the whole world, for victory of the world revolution." Signed by secretary of the group Fanny P.

Fanny P. was a hyperactive person. While in Karelia we kids got to know her as our dancing teacher. Even the dances had an ideological flavor, one of them was a revolutionary dance dedicated to the memory of Isadora Duncan. What a flop our performance turned out to be! This is how it happened. A festival of amateur dance groups was under way at the Petrozavodsk culture park. Knowing we had a performance on Sunday at 12:00, we nevertheless decided to go to Devil's Chair, a beautiful recreation spot across the bay from Petrozavodsk, for Midsummer. Well the warmth, the sunning, swimming, walking and running got the better of us and we overslept the bus that was to take us back to town from Solomennoye, so we just had to walk it. On top of the overexertion from Devil's Chair we had a nice hike and getting home, fell into a deep slumber at Inga Honka's place. I don't even remember who awoke us. All we heard was, "You've got to be at the park in half an hour." Another hike and when we finally got there, Fanny was kindling with wrath. The music began playing and she literally pushed us on stage. Oh, well, it's not hard to imagine those deprived of all plasticity "dancers" who only insulted the worthy memory of

A 1932 group on board the Gripshholm. The group is made up mostly of Midwesterners.

Isadora Duncan. But Fanny would never forgive us and she cut her dancing teacher's career short.

In the States and in Karelia I've talked with Americans who were 15–18 at the time of the crossings. They have only a few laudatory remarks to describe their feelings, "Great! Wonderful! Exciting!" The travellers had lots of fun on board: improvised concerts, dances, games. All the activities they were accustomed to in the Halls back home were put to the test. They aroused the admiration of many tourists and one of them even made up his mind to follow the would-be Karelians to their place of destination. There's a paper proving this fact in the KRA materials: Armas Orre is applying for a visa to be sent to him to Helsinki. Satisfaction with the voyage can be judged of by a lengthy letter of commendation to SAL authorities. The passengers thanked them for the excellent food, cabins and service.

Fun doesn't last forever. The grey panorama of Leningrad that opened to them, the overnight tedious ride from there to Petrozavodsk on a dirty train poured cold water on the spirits of many. But still hopes were running high, maybe first impressions wouldn't be lasting and as soon as they get settled down a normal life would follow? Probably not so well-provided for as back home, but... "Let's take the good with the bad," they thought. "While there's life, there's hope!"

3 There

A view of Petrozavodsk, circa 1935

First impressions were greatly dependent on how the night had passed in the inconvenient train and on the time of the year. Of course, many had their noses glued to the window on hearing that they were approaching Petrozavodsk but the dirty windows made it next to impossible to see anything; only an all-grey panorama prevailed. But if the weather was favorable, you could make out a big lake on the shores of which the one-story town of old black houses was scattered. But for the size it was more reminiscent of a village: only a few high rises.

The most unlucky were those who arrived on a gloomy late autumn morning with overcast skies and muddy roads: there really were no paved streets or sidewalks. The station was very forbidding, so one and all were eager to get away from there as soon as possible. The short trip to the barracks, to where they were taken, was either by truck or on horse-drawn carts: no buses, no street cars, to say nothing of private cars owned by those who had come to wish them welcome. Yes, barracks, such was the housing the arrivals had to put up with for quite a time: the Station barracks, the Golikovka barracks, the Uritski barracks—long squat buildings with just as long a hallway and doors opening to rooms on both sides. It often happened that arrivals even had to share a room—two, three families in one. No running water, no sewage (the outhouses were round the corner), no central heating and more often than not the rooms were already inhabited: by little living creatures—roaches and bedbugs. An acquaintance recalled that the first American song they heard someone singing was from the mining and lumbering days in America, "They go wild simply wild over me. I'm referring to the bed-bugs and the fleas. They disturb my slumber deep and I murmur in my sleep: They go wild, simply wild over me."

Not everyone could take it. There were those who never unpacked, never registered for employment, never handed in their papers for registration, just turned back as soon as the ticket arrangements were made. Such was the decision of five women and two men, who arrived on August 1, 1932 and, I'm sure, they weren't the only ones: hundreds had come before them and nothing had changed for the better! Decisive collective action of the kind caused quite a stir, that's why such departure cases are even registered in the Resettling Management papers. It was evident that if Karelia didn't expect to see the end of immigration then and there something had to be done and urgently. Better housing, although also lacking in conveniences, began appearing due to the American construction workers themselves. It would take two-score years for conveniences to appear gradually. We've all gone through it: first running water and heat, then gas (later electric) ranges, then running hot water.

For many these barracks turned out to be temporary, as, after receiving their assignments, the immigrants had to go to other places. The 1931 plan for inviting American labor was the following:

construction workers	522
drivers and tractor-drivers	19
mechanics	25
blacksmiths	13
workers for agriculture and forestry	143
miners	10
masons	10
smelters	3
miscellany	10
	785

(As compared to an earlier plan for recruiting 1000 loggers for 1931, the number here seems revised, although there's no indication of the fact in the paper).

Those who had already arrived by July 19, 1931 were distributed to the following places:

	men	women	children	total
Petrozavodsk	220	98	59	377
Kondopoga	50	10	10	70
Hiilisuo (agro)	10	8	10	28
Matrosa (logging)	58	27	4	90
Vilga (logging)	33	16	5	54
Aunus (agro and sawmill)	5	4	10	19
Kem (sawmill)	11	10	4	25
Uhtua	1			1
TOTAL	388	173	102	663

It goes without saying that these 663, and some of the earlier arrivals, were the more fortunate ones: the majority landed in towns or in settlements situated not far from Petrozavodsk. This implied a quicker improvement of living conditions, including food supplies as the capital of the Republic had the "Insnab" and "Torgsin" stories.

Working and living in Petrozavodsk with the Onega tractor plant, ski factory, sawmill, Karelavto (Karjalan Auto) and several building trusts, or in Kondopoga with the huge paper and pulp mill expanding, a building trust was considered good luck. The work was professional and pay was higher. So it wasn't by chance that when "recruiters" from these places offered jobs to Americans in other parts of the Republic, it didn't take them long to win the workers over. But this practice was censured by the authorities as it created fall-behinds in production plans of the enterprise left behind. There was another disadvantage for the foreigners which they didn't realize at the time. Voluntary moving from one work place to another told on the well-being of the person concerned: he was not refunded the passage fare, tools or equipment he had handed over to the enterprise to which he had been appointed.

A few words about refunding, so as not to return to this issue, which, as many others, proved to be unfortunate. I've touched upon the fact that future emigres gave Karelia substantial material support. I failed to find new illustrations to this item in the archives and remain a supporter of the data provided by Prof. Reino Kero in his outstanding "Neuvosto-Karjalaa Rakentamassa." The overwhelming majority of Americans entering the country under the auspices of the KTA donated money to the "Konerahasto"

("Machine fund"). Some of these donations were in four-figure numbers, a few in five-figures: Pekka Katainen, Joonas Harju. Thus there's no need to doubt that the total really amounted to millions of dollars.[10]

Also, we shouldn't lose sight of the fact that the contract provided for the refunding of passage fares, the cost of tools and equipment handed over to the enterprise where the worker was to work with his own tools, as well as for excess tools or equipment which an immigrant had the legal right to sell (at the same rate $1 = 2 rubles). Judging by documents (KCPS decision of May 14, 1931 "On the refunding of workers' expenses by enterprises involved in importing qualified foreign labor") this government obligation had not been forgotten, but reality goes to prove that mandatory compensation was not happening.

Some of my correspondents produced receipts, certifying sums their family had donated which were never refunded, especially in cases where the receipt-holder had passed through NKVD portals: Hjalmar Tarvainen, Lauri Laitinen, Karl Hakanen, Viktor Nikander. Papers exist which prove that there even were returnees who had not been refunded (the sums are not indicated) and, since they were informed that sending currency out of the country was impossible, they were recommended to bank it. In this way Leino (Petrozavodsk) and Sirola (Moscow) received several proxies authorizing them to dispose of the deposited money in the best way they see fit to alleviate the circumstances of those remaining and in helping to raise productivity. Sounds like big money!

The later arrivals were in less favorable conditions as they landed in far-off places where the living conditions were worse and where no immediate improvements were visible: Uhtua, with its highly productive Kannussuo logging camp (it practically came to a standstill in 1938 when about 50% of the loggers were arrested); another Uhtua camp Kieskis was affectionately called Kiss-Kiss by a romantic; Luulampi in the Tunkua district; Repola and Rukajärvi in the Louhi district. The logging camps Interposyolok, Matrosa, Lososinnoye, Pai and Paatjärvi were not considered bad places due to their proximity to Petrozavodsk and other close-by settlements with lots of Finns. There was another advantage: as there were no old barracks on the spot, the Finns put up houses out of fresh pine and the exquisite natural scents were healthy too.

There were numerous problems that complicated life. One of them was that the travelling pattern "first husband, then wife and kids" had suffered a backlash. The Soviet government showed no concern in separating families. The main aim of the authorities was achieved: the men were putting in hours in the forests, on construction sites, in factories and mills. Less need to be troubled with the complex problems of housing and occupation! But the workers wouldn't put up with it: they threatened to give up their jobs and return to America (those who had stuck to their foreign passports). Numerous messages were dispatched by Karelian authorities to the Russian Ministry of Foreign Affairs, requesting that visas for wives and children be sped up.

In one of these letters, dated September 1, 1931, Chairman Gylling wrote, "141 Americans haven't been granted visas. They are mostly wives and children of men who are already here. Their spirits are low. Such a situation hinders further recruiting. Many Americans have already set off on the trip to Soviet Russia. They are left stranded for weeks awaiting visas in Stockholm or Revel." Needless to say the firm stand taken by the men and supported by the Karelian government yielded fruit. Moscow's intervention bore another result too—so-called group visas. Several of them were issued in 1933—NN 703041, 702999, 702916. But by this time emigration from America had dwindled down, so the effect was belated. But this could serve as an example to show how much time it took for the bureaucratic machine to get going.

Another problem was dealing with the customs. The customs had their orders: these were people coming to work by contract, so they should get most-favored nation treatment. Nothing of the kind! There was barely a group that didn't count customs losses, especially in personal goods. But customs officers didn't stop at that: they also confiscated goods brought into the country in keeping with preliminary agreement with the Karelian government, goods that were to enhance the economic process. KRA papers contain several letters addressed to Central customs offices to this effect. One of them deals with five boxes of goods purchased by Theodore Hautala at his own expense to use for the installation of a long-wave broadcasting station that was already going up in Petrozavodsk. The equipment soon arrived, Teddy Hautala got the coveted job and Petrozavodsk—a new radio station.

If someone reading these lines can recall such an undignified, embarrassing experience of his own, let me set you at ease; such was the lot of all legal border-crossers way up to the eighties, unless you were a VIP of some sort, throwing your weight around. But the customs, like everywhere else, had the "good guys" and the "bad guys." When you got into the hands of the former, what a relief! Once I had to do repacking all the way from the border to Leningrad! The Devil knows what the officer was looking for!

Another thing the Finns couldn't digest was the way they were kept tabs on, their having no right to move from one place to another in search of better living and working conditions. Those who had not taken Soviet citizenship, were obliged to make a monthly appearance at the passport department and answer the same old questions, but now new ones were added, "What kind of socially active work do you perform? What's your opinion about the working conditions?" It's hard to say how some Finns had found themselves in distant parts of the country. They had arrived earlier with KTA groups but were now returning to Karelia from Baku (Herman Copper), from Kanavino (Karl Lahti), Will J. from Dagestan, where he had been helping the locals set up a fish cannery. In his letter to Karelia he wrote, "I was not escaping unemployment leaving America." Eight families came from Siberia. There was quite a wide exchange between Nizhny Novgorod, to where the "Cement" groups had gone straight from New York, and Karelia, six single men left for Leningrad, a huge group set off for the Far East. All these moves went through the Resettling Management.

Way into the eighties foreigners were taken aback by the vast number of armed military that were walking the streets. It seemed as if the country was at war. This was shocking to the arrivals of the thirties, but yet in 1986, when the first Duluthians showed up in Petrozavodsk, one of the questions we heard was, "Why are there so many soldiers and officers parading the streets? Is something going on?" You probably know that even today cutting down on the military is a vital government issue. Russia has far from rid itself of people who still nurture the enemy vision and insist on maintaining a large army. Nevertheless the street scene has noticeably changed for the better in this respect.

Finnish-Americans were quick to grasp essential differences existing in the organization of labor and government in Russia as compared to America. "The one man—no choice" principle was mind-boggling. It was manifest everywhere: whether a government official was being elected, or a trade union boss. Higher up on the ladder "the one man" was already agreed upon. It only remained to raise your hand in the voting procedure and that's that! As labor experience showed, this "one and only" was not the most efficient, competent man. Beyond doubt he possessed other qualities which satisfied the VIP's.

Americans thought they were coming to a country where class distinctions had been eliminated. That, perhaps, was one of the most deluding notions. Nowhere was there such a privileged class as that of the nomenklatura in Russia and its vassal countries. Of course they tried to conceal their priorities, but it didn't work. You just had to be blind not to notice what was going on: better housing, higher salaries, choice food supplies at special stores or at special hours in smaller places. This system found classified development (four groups of rations) and would never have ended but for the country's attempts to pass over to a market economy. There's no need for them to be buying at lower cost today, because the former nomenklatura has the money!

But the Finnish-American immigrants with their American-earned experience in class struggle and trade unionism wouldn't put up with this. There are numerous examples in the papers that prove how American workers had interfered with privileges in paying workers and bosses (Lososinnoye), how they had exposed the incompetence and indifference of local bosses. One of the most striking examples is that of how these immigrant workers intervened knowing that a brick-making factory bought in the US and brought over by a group had been standing idle at the station for nine months. And this at a time when the country was in dire need of construction materials! This factory alone was capable of producing 17,000 bricks per hour. Try as I did, I couldn't trace where the brick factory finally landed. Hopefully in Solomennoye or in a place which today is called "Kirpichny zavod" (Brick factory). Several years later death sentences for "praising capitalist reality" and daring to find fault with the system were passed on hundreds. That is how their criticism was qualified. If there had been a possibility to fight for better living and working conditions in the open, it would have helped. But little by little criticism subsided and turned into the "kitchen talk" that lasted up to the death of Stalin and was picked up again after the Khrushchev "thaw" ended. Good that Gorbachev came along when he did.

But still criticism was not for nothing. Two capital inspections of living conditions were conducted at the initiative of foreign workers in Lososinnoye and Luulampi. It looks as if they had lodged their complaints with "Moscow Daily News": an editor from there, Swarstein by name, had participated in the survey and his estimation of the situation was objective. Luulampi: "food is poor and insufficient, no possibility to grow food, as the land is marshy and rocky, housing very poor, no conditions to weather the winter." He gave high praise to Brunila's brigade. Lososinnoye: "Workers are overcharged for food which is of poor quality. In Lososinnoye workers pay 120 rubles a month, as compared to 53 R in Kuzbass, 75 R in Prokopyevsk. Living conditions are poor. No idea how the workers are expected to live through the winter." Leino from the Labor Commissariat proposed a number of urgent measures, but on reading the words of the Lososinnoye camp chief engineer Kirpetski, I got the creeps, "We built the BBK (White Sea Canal) without the help of foreign workers and it's an excellent canal." There's some reading on this point in the next chapter.

No doubt conditions were hard and they gave rise to the departure of hundreds.

Here is the official data of departures given by the Resettling Management for the years 1933, 1934, 1935:

	US	Canada	Total
1933	533	216	749
1934	220	169	389
1935	138	70	208
	891	455	1346

These figures are substantiated by names.

Thus we may judge that arrivals from the US had greater chances of returning to America than those who had arrived to Russia from Canada. Undoubtedly it was a financial problem, as we know that a substantial part of the immigrants from Canada were unmarried men, men who had come face to face with the loss of jobs.

One should think after all that has been said, Americans working in Russia would have seen light. But no! The ideological impact was still very strong. Here's an extract from a letter Kalle Heino sent to KTA in July 1931. "Things here are OK. The guys are having some stomach problems. Living conditions are squashed. We have enough food and we're working. Many are on the verge of returning to America from here, but there is a majority of those who wouldn't return even if they got a free trip back. The understanding of the situation is so varied. Everything depends on the level of a person's political consciousness."

Karelian newspapers qualified the criticism of Karelia that appeared in Finnish-American papers, thanks to those who had returned, as "petty lies about the socialist way of life." This opinion was fortified by a letter of Luulammi workers. Here's an extract: "We American workers, who came to Luulammi, condemn those who were given a comradely welcome but then became purposeful or incidental smearers of the Soviet Union and the Karelian working class. We declare that we are free Soviet citizens and are working hard due to our own free will and we don't agree with the counter-revolutionary tales about our forced labor in trying conditions. We stress that our living quarters and other conditions are quite satisfactory and unanimously condemn the kulak supporters, who spread false rumors and in this way serve the interests of fascists and other counter-revolutionary elements." Dated April 19, 1932. Adopted at a general workers' meeting.

But thousands stayed. We stayed. Were the minds of all those who stayed muddled in the same way? No. But when people are honest and hard-working they don't let the circumstances get the better of them. They look forward to a happier future. Many built families, had children, worked for the common good and are rightfully proud of their contribution to that multi-suffering land called Russia. Finnish-Americans can also be proud of the philosophical impact they've had on those they rubbed shoulders with. I'd like to share some of the highest praise I've ever received. It came from Natasha Bogomazova, a former student of mine. She's now mother of two high-school students and a distinguished teacher at School N 17 where the students major in English. This conversation took place in the street about a year ago, in English, naturally.

Natasha: "Oh. Mayme Oscarovna, I'm so happy to see you."

Mayme: "So am I. It's always a treat to meet you grown-up kids."

Natasha: "Let me ask you a question, "do you know why I and masses of others came to the foreign language department?"

Mayme: "I'll always remember you as a linguist, a language lover."

Natasha: "True, but that's not it. We came to the department because it was an oasis of democracy in the city."

Mayme: "Thank you, Natasha, you've made my day!"

Natasha: "And then I landed in your brother's school. How fortunate I am!"

Yes, Finnish-Americans were an oasis of democracy in Russia. We were not better, but we were different. We had preserved the humane qualities instilled in us during a happy childhood by our schooling and honest dedicated parents who would not have been capable of putting their signatures under a letter of lies, like the one quoted above. We have our ideals. You cannot live without ideals! We have tried not to put up with the injustices practiced in our places of occupation, in the current policy of the state. We have been outspoken and have often wondered how it is that our "betters" have put up with us. But our ideals have nothing to do with the dangerous philosophy of communism that throughout the world is destroying millions physically and poisoning their minds.

I wasn't stretching a point writing about our elders, about my peers in "Red Exodus." That's the way it was. Our losses were tragic and heavy but we don't have to say, "Our lives have been wasted." No, they'll bear fruit just like the seeds planted in us by our idealistic parents, whom we love. And our followers will keep the torch burning too!

4 Graveland

Karelia with its pristine forests and numerous fresh water sources was so much like the Finland our forefathers had left behind 30–40 years ago, others, only 5–10 years before departure to Russia. Every person had had his own reasons for leaving Suomi, and now its closeness to Karelia was inspiring. The similarity of Karelia with Old Finland was evident in the low living standards: the same poverty, a lack of normal dwellings, conveniences and food, an absolute absence of roads and, consequently, transportation. Such was the parallel drawn by those who had arrived to America in the early 20th century and even in the twenties. But immigrants to America also remembered their achievements: houses of their own, good furniture, cars, the Halls which made workers' and their families' recreation so rewarding. So, they thought, they could do the same here: they knew how to work. It wouldn't take them too long with the experience acquired in America and the instruments and tools they brought along from the New World to prove their worth.

There was another thing immigrants to Russia stressed both on the way there and during the first days of their life in Soviet Russia: freedom and equality. Here, they thought, nobody was going to persecute them for their political convictions, force them to go on strike, consider the Finns so much beneath immigrants from other countries, blacklist them. With freedom and equality their efforts would be crowned with success and they'd prove what they were capable of!

But they had another guess coming.

Undoubtedly the present-day aspect of Karelia, especially its capital Petrozavodsk, has changed for the better. Numerous Finnish-American families, too, began enjoying the benefits of a civilized life. They moved into apartments in high-rises. The families that were better-off built summer cottages (dachas) and bought cars. Only... Only... Only the number of people who survived to enjoy all these pleasantries is all together too small, recalling the thousands of Finns from America and the even greater number of people from Finland who had arrived in the twenties and thirties to give the country the badly needed economic boost.

Notwithstanding the indisputable merits of Mother Nature my lengthy research makes me regard Karelia in another light—in the light of a huge graveland. The pristine forests have been reduced to a fraction of what they used to be, the lakes and rivers are polluted. Walking in the woods, growing in place of a ravished forest with only stumps to show what massive trees used to grow there, I always caught myself thinking: I wonder whose grave I'm walking on!

I dare say, without any danger of exaggeration, that you couldn't find another part of the country, huge territories of which were ravaged by Nazi hordes, where the number of people buried per kilometer of ground would be higher. Of course, no measurements have ever been made, nor can they ever be made. There are so many graves that bear no crosses or any other signs to indicate that someone is buried here, and in most cases not just one victim but masses!

Facts, only facts could prove my point. I'll use the ones I have, but I've reason to believe my materials on Karelia are far from the total that exist, and some day new ones will hopefully be brought to light by more successful researchers.

Today that is already happening on a country-wide scale. Outstanding Russian scientists have finally gained access to central formerly top-secret archive materials and they are unearthing new names of thousands and thousands of victims. I've already introduced my readers to the names of Dmitri Volkogonov, Edward Radzinsky and Arkady Vaxberg. Dm. Volkogonov passed away recently after a serious illness. Certain "politicians" heaved a sigh of relief at his demise. Why? Because he was dealing with facts that left no doubt as to the true nature of the Bolshevik revolution, to the essence of its leaders—Lenin, Stalin and Trotsky, whose principal tool in "class struggle" was terror!

Terror became the official policy of the state after Stalin's speech at the July 1928 plenary session of the Central Committee of the Russian Communist Party (bolsheviks), as the Communist party was then called. Stalin's thesis was, in short, that the closer the country approaches socialism, the more acute class struggle would be. If this was not a direct appeal to launch a campaign of arrests and beheadings, it was certainly interpreted as such when Moscow gave the go-ahead with mass arrests in the center.

The evil of genocide has not died. There are people all over the world who close their eyes to this ugly fact. Are you aware of the post-war appearance of books, claiming there had been no concentration camps, no mass exterminations in Germany? Today similar opinions are being voiced in Russia: there was no Stalinist terror: if some people languished in prison or were executed, they deserved it. Such opinions pour water on the mill of extremists and terrorists of all makes. God! How dangerous!

As compared to global problems my topic is a narrow one. But I'm convinced it's no less important, as it deals with people whose memory is still green, people who still have kin that are mourning their loss, people with friends of days gone but not forgotten. And, as you'll see, I couldn't overlook other crimes committed in Karelia, crimes which are not connected with the fates of Finnish-Americans, but with natives of the country that was called the Union of Soviet Socialist Republics.

Back to my statement. On what grounds do I make the assertion that Karelia could be called a graveland? Are these months and years remindful of anything?

The 1920's.

The 1930's.

December 1939–March 1940.

June 1941–May 1945.

Let's decipher this:

The 1920's. This is when undisguised forced labor was introduced in the country. It led to a precisely unknown number of deaths that would be no less than a million. The first-ever Russian gulags appeared on Karelian territory.

The 1930's. This was the height of Stalinist repressions, that carried away millions of lives, tens of thousands in Karelia;

December 1939–March 1940. The Winter War. The true number of victims remains to be established;

June 1941–May 1945. World War II, or the Great Patriotic War: over

80,000 soldiers and officers buried in Karelia.

Graves! Graves! Graves!

THE TWENTIES.

Take a look at the map. You'll see that from Lake Onega there's a waterway connecting Karelian ports with the five seas: the Belomorsk-Baltic Canal, abbreviated BBK. ("Canal" in Russian is spelled with a "K." In English literature the Canal is usually referred to as the The White Sea Canal or the White Sea-Baltic Canal). For Soviet citizens the abbreviation BBK was foremostly accepted as the name of the first huge-scale gulag in the country, as the canal itself was built by forced labor. Cutting through the cliffs characteristic of the landscape involved wasn't easy: the builders died like flies. Numerous books have been written and there's a great documentary about the BBK, too. Seeing those poor people pushing heavy wheel-barrows along shaky platforms, you get the creeps. There are a few close-ups and you catch a glimpse of a smiling man or woman ("Smile or die!") emptying the wheel-barrow into the pit of the future canal. Knowing the truth is terrifying. The Solovki Islands in the White Sea (formerly Karelian territory, now Solovki belong to the Arkhangel region) became the final destination for the survivor-builders and thousands more were to come to other camps. These islands with their beautiful monastery and churches became a horrendous gulag from where the only escape was death or magic release for a few, like e.g. Academician Dmitri Likhachev, whose contribution to solving the "mysteries" of the BBK and Solovki is enormous.

Today Solovki is one of the major tourist attractions in Northern Russia and visitors enraptured by the surrounding beauty are apt to be so carried away by it that the tragic past might remain in the shadows. It's estimated that about 800,000 men and women were left in the wake of the canal. You'll find no graves. They say that corpses were thrown to the bottom of the future canal and topped with reinforced concrete! Will such graves ever be found? Eight hundred thousand.

The number of Finnish-Americans in the country was small, but the role they played in the national economy was instrumental. They were spared at the time. (the followers of Trincher, the agricultural and fishing communes in the Rostov region—"Kylväjä," on the White Sea coast—the Knösäs, in Karelia—"Säde," in the Leningrad region—"Työ").[11]

THE THIRTIES.

The illegal arrests made a huge sweep of honest laborers, including those who had come from America. They began "disappearing" in the summer of 1937, although a few had fallen victim even earlier, e.g. Kalle Stolt.

The figures of purge victims I gave in "Red Exodus" were based only on letters and interviews with survivors of the immigrant families. It was obvious that they could not be considered exhaustive as, judging by statements of former fellow-workers, so many still remained to be found. Besides, as it turned out, there were hundreds about whom I had no idea. Today the "Red Exodus" figures are greatly outdated!

So where did new ones come from?

The first actual names to appear were published in rehabilitation lists submitted by NKVD and made up by the Petrozavodsk Memorial Society.[12] Then followed "The Martyrologue" compiled and published in the local paper "Petrozavodsk" thanks to the efforts of Ivan Chukhin, parliamentarian from Karelia. He's the man my circle of people voted for in December 1995, too. But, unfortunately, he wasn't re-elected: too down-to-earth, realistic and objective a man. A democrat to the marrow of the bone! Chukhin made it his business to see that victims of Stalinism were brought to the attention of his electorate, to see to their belated rehabilitation. That, as we know, is not in everyone's interests.

But only when I finally got to the NKVDA was I overwhelmed by the flood of information. That information came from three different kinds of papers:

First, copies of sentences dished out in 1937–1938.

Second, protocols of sentences put into effect.

Third, personal files. As to the first two types of papers, they will be dealt with separately in the following chapters. I'll now dwell on personal files.

As a rule, personal files are given only to relatives of the victim and only after they have been examined by the Prosecutor's office for the purpose of rehabilitation. Agreeing with my request in conformity with the research I was conducting, supported by the Science department of Petrozavodsk University, I was given the chance to study the files of Matti Tenhunen, Kalle Aronen and my father Oscar Corgan—the principal US actors in the tragedy called "The Emigration of Finnish-Americans to Soviet Russia." Notes in Father's file compelled me to ask for Emil Salonen's. I wasn't refused. I also asked for information on an American lad from New

Jersey, the USA. Pekka was the only son of Ingrid and Väinö Kanto. I did not get his file but an officer read for me out of it. I learned that early in the war Lieutenant Pekka Kanto had been arrested (that accounts for his file being in the NKVDA) on the charge "of not having reported on the intentional crossing of the front line to the Finnish side of a soldier." After all these years it's evident we'll see no more of this handsome upright young man. The next and last we'll hear about him will be a rehabilitation notice to appear (when???) in Memorial papers.

The reading of one file was a working day in itself, not because it was so thick, but because it was so incomprehensible and often even ludicrous.

Superior, Wisconsin is the place where it all began. The key figure of organizing emigration to Russia was Matti Tenhunen, an educated man, a good speaker well-known among Finnish Americans in the Midwest and on the Eastern coast, but entirely unknown among the population of Karelia, regardless of all his positive efforts for the benefit of the republic. The Tenhunens were our family friends. Irma, three years older than myself, was one I always looked up to. Toivo, her big brother, was quick to break with the communist movement after his short stay in Russia where his family went in 1931. Regarding Toivo's riff with the family, which occurred on an ideological basis, it crosses my mind that probably young people have a better understanding of reality and it would be worthwhile to heed their opinions, to hear them out. Toivo's firm conviction was that nothing would come of the Soviet experiment and that Americans were putting their heads in a noose. In NKVD papers he's called a renegade. But he turned out to be right!

File F/P 5045. Matti Tenhunen. Military Collegium of USSR Supreme Court, presentation of case by NKVD, Karelian ASSR, about counter-revolutionary activities of Tenhunen, signed by Tenison, People's Commissar of Internal Affairs, Karelian ASSR. Decision about expulsion from All-Union Communist Party (bolsheviks), dated Sept. 21, 1937.

Further: Tenhunen was accused of anti-Soviet activities in the US in favor of Finland; of taking advantage of the position he occupied for three months in New York, appointed by the Karelian People's Commissariat of Labor to recruit anti-Soviet inclined people to Soviet Russia; organizing anti-Soviet activity in Karelia.

Tenhunen denied his guilt outright.

Being the key figure that he was, the number of people (most of them already among the arrested, e.g. Forsten, Gylling, Rovio, Vilmi and others) mentioned in his file was high. One of the witnesses, an American Finn by the way, took advantage of the rift between father and son, insinuating that a decent father couldn't have a son who did not support the Soviet Union.

On December 1, 1955, this 100-page file was returned to the Military Prosecutor of the Northern Military Circuit for rehabilitation. The final paper in M.Tenhunen's file is Irma's receipt confirming she had received her father's rehabilitation papers. That was January 22, 1958. A year later I was lucky enough to visit her and son in their beautiful Moscow home. Irma has joined the silent majority but her son remains. "Red Exodus," which I sent him, was actually the first chance he had to learn about his grandpa and the turbulent life of Finnish-Americans who had come to Russia.

File N P-7070. Kalle Aronen. It might seem incredible to the reader that my writings are often accompanied by personal reminiscences of people. But it really was so. The Aronens became our very good friends as soon as we arrived in New York where Father was to take over the Karelian Technical Aid as the Aronens were soon departing for Russia. They were great folks and it pains me to recall Hilma, left all alone, with only friends surrounding her, on her death-bed in Shuyeretskoe, Kem district Karelia, where I saw her last. That was in 1942, war-time.

The accusations were the same, but in this file special stress is laid on Aronen's activities in recruiting spies to the Soviet Union already in New York and maintaining counter-revolutionary contacts with them in Karelia in favor of Finland.

The files I read yielded several new names, e.g. Karl Leppänen, b.12.03.1888. He is mentioned as one of Aronen's contact persons, but this is the only available information on him. I can just imagine how many more Finnish-Americans I'd find if it were possible to read all their files. But, as mentioned they were not available. Hopefully somebody else will do it!

File FP 4641. Salonen Emil Gustavovich, b.1896, Tampere. This file was interesting for two reasons: first, he was one of the many who had become an anti-Soviet agent already in New York, recruited by Corgan. There is a protocol in the file describing a cross-examination with Aronen on July 27, 1938. The talk was about a meeting in Corgan's home in 1935 (Petrozavodsk), where it was decided to pass over to organizing diversive acts at the largest industrial enterprises of the Republic. "Corgan's proposal was to commit these acts in 1938." Second, Emil and Anna Salonen had a 1925 US-born boy, Fred by name, who crossed the front line in WWII to the Finnish side. In Emil's file there's indication of the fact that Fred had returned from prison and his father's rehabilitation papers were sent to him to the address: Pitkaranta, Lenin St.14,7. Thus it was logical to draw the conclusion that he had been returned to the country as a POW on conditions of the peace treaty and paid "for his crime" with the years of his youth, like so many others, in a gulag. This conclusion was later confirmed in Finland's military archives.

First I just looked at Father's file lying on the table: the only thing that remained of him! I tried to imagine what I'd find there. I even expected to find our birth certificates, the very ones that had been confiscated when they led Dad away. (Up to this day we cannot get Paul's; he's just not on record in Hancock, Michigan, where he was born March 14, 1925). No birth certificates!

I took my courage into both hands, swept away the tears swimming in my eyes and began reading.

File N P-3305. The indictment, if it can be called so, since there was no trial, was made in the presence of Iivari Järvi on the basis of information presented by... The name of the informer was crossed out. The charges were numerous:

expulsion from the Communist party of America (this had actually happened and was correspondingly confirmed by Corgan);

promoting the infiltration of Karelia with fascist agents of Finland's secret service; the guiding principle for recruiting people to Karelia was anti-Sovietism; preference was shown for people with small businesses (petit bourgeois);

the sales of a brochure written by enemy of the people Irklis (Karelia's regional party secretary after the arrest of Rovio. Arrested and liquidated in the summer of 1937, shortly after the execution of Rovio); membership and leadership in the IWW (acknowledged); racism displayed in derogatory statements about blacks (Probably, that's why we Corgan kids went to schools for blacks in Harlem); the forceful Russification of schools in Karelia (Finnish was being ousted!) and nationalism; counter-revolutionary propaganda.

Interrogation was first carried on in Uhtua, the place of arrest, later by officers of the Leningrad regional NKVD, but the place is not indicated.

Every accusation was followed by the question, "Do you admit your guilt?" "No," was the answer but as to nationalism, this requires a quote from the file, "Yes, I admit having made statements about my disagreement with the nationalist policy of the Soviet Union and its Communist party."

Enough to be hanged! Not a syllable of criticism in the address of the regime was ever tolerated.

Another important detail characterizing human nature that I discovered in Father's file was the reaction of former friends to the problem of rehabilitation. This process began after Khrushchev's 1956 exposures. Letters started pouring in to government officials, prosecutors' offices and NKVD demanding that the honor of innocent victims be restored.

Judging by what I read in the four files there are a few items it pays to generalize on:

First, every single person is accused of activities conducted in favor of the Intelligence Service of Finland. In the United States and Canada Tenhunen, Aronen, Corgan and Latva were recruiting future emigrants on behalf of the Intelligence Service of Finland. They correspondingly maintained contacts with Finland's agents in the US. There is no mention whatsoever of any kind of activity in favor of US or Canadian Intelligence services. The same relates to ALL other papers connected with the arrests of Finnish-Americans. E.g. from Oscar Corgan's file: "Protocol N 9. January 2, 1938. Those present: USSR People's Commissar of Internal Affairs (NKVD); USSR Prosecutor. Heard: Materials relating to persons connected with espionage and diversive activities in favor of Finland, presented by NKVD of Karelian ASSR, Decision N 17. Oscar Frederick Karlovich Corgan, b.1887, Sweden, to be shot. Authenticity of copy confirmed by Blazhevich, 7.02.56." It stands to reason that there are no personal signatures of the high-standing dignitaries mentioned in Protocol N 9. With mass executions going on in the country those VIP's would have been doing nothing else but signing death sentences!

Second, the activities conducted by the New York and Toronto Karelian Technical Agencies allegedly had one main objective: to recruit forces to Soviet Russia which would help to overthrow the government of the Soviets.

Third, there is a discrepancy in the documents which allows to contend that the exact number of executed will not be established for a long, long time. That will be possible only after EVERY case-file is seriously considered by researchers. That is why I attach such great importance to the work conducted by I. Chukhin and his assistants and the "Memorial" society which is working on this issue.

Fourth, when sentences were undergoing re-examination and rehabilitation was underway, questions pertaining to the honor and respectability of each person under consideration were put to citizens who had known the person. I was happy to read the evidence of Viola Nikula (Oulu, Wisconsin) Anna Sutinen (New York), Paraskeva Lobskaya-Barskaya, deputy Minister of education in Karelia and Yevdokia Salonen (Uhtua). The latter rejected "evidence" she was forced to give in 1937 under pressure. But another lady, a friend from New York, who was a frequent visitor in our family on both sides of the ocean, claimed she didn't know Oscar Corgan well enough to say this or that. Oh, well! She was an active party member in Petrozavodsk and she just wasn't taking any chances. What if things began falling back into place?

The "Memorial" society is not subsidized. The nouveau rich could donate to the worthy cause of establishing the innocence and restoring the honor of victims of communism, but it hasn't happened yet and, I'm afraid it won't. If the situation remains the same and this huge important historic mission is destined to remain in the hands of enthusiasts, it'll take scores of years and disappear in the sands of time. That would only play into the hands of reactionaries and terrorists.

The White Sea Canal from Onega Bay of the White Sea at Belomorsk passes along lower canalized Vyg River through Lake Vyg Ozero, and across 240 feet-high watershed (using 19 locks) to Lake Onega at Povenets—140 miles long. (The data given in the upper frame is now outdated as new information has surfaced.) Karelia had the "honor" of the first gulags (forced labor camps).

LABOR CAMPS IN EUROPEAN RUSSIA 1917–1936

In February 1917 a spontaneous amnesty led to the release of all Tsarist political prisoners and exiles. Many returned from the remote corners of Russia to play a prominent part in the Bolshevik revolution. But the Bolsheviks themselves soon began sending their opponents and critics to forced labor camps (Corrective Labor Colonies). By 1930 there were an estimated minimum of 750,000 prisoners employed by the CHEKA (later OGPU), the Soviet political and security police. Conditions were as bad as they had been in Tsarist times for political prisoners sent to the Kara Mines, and were far worse than for the majority of Tsarist exiles.

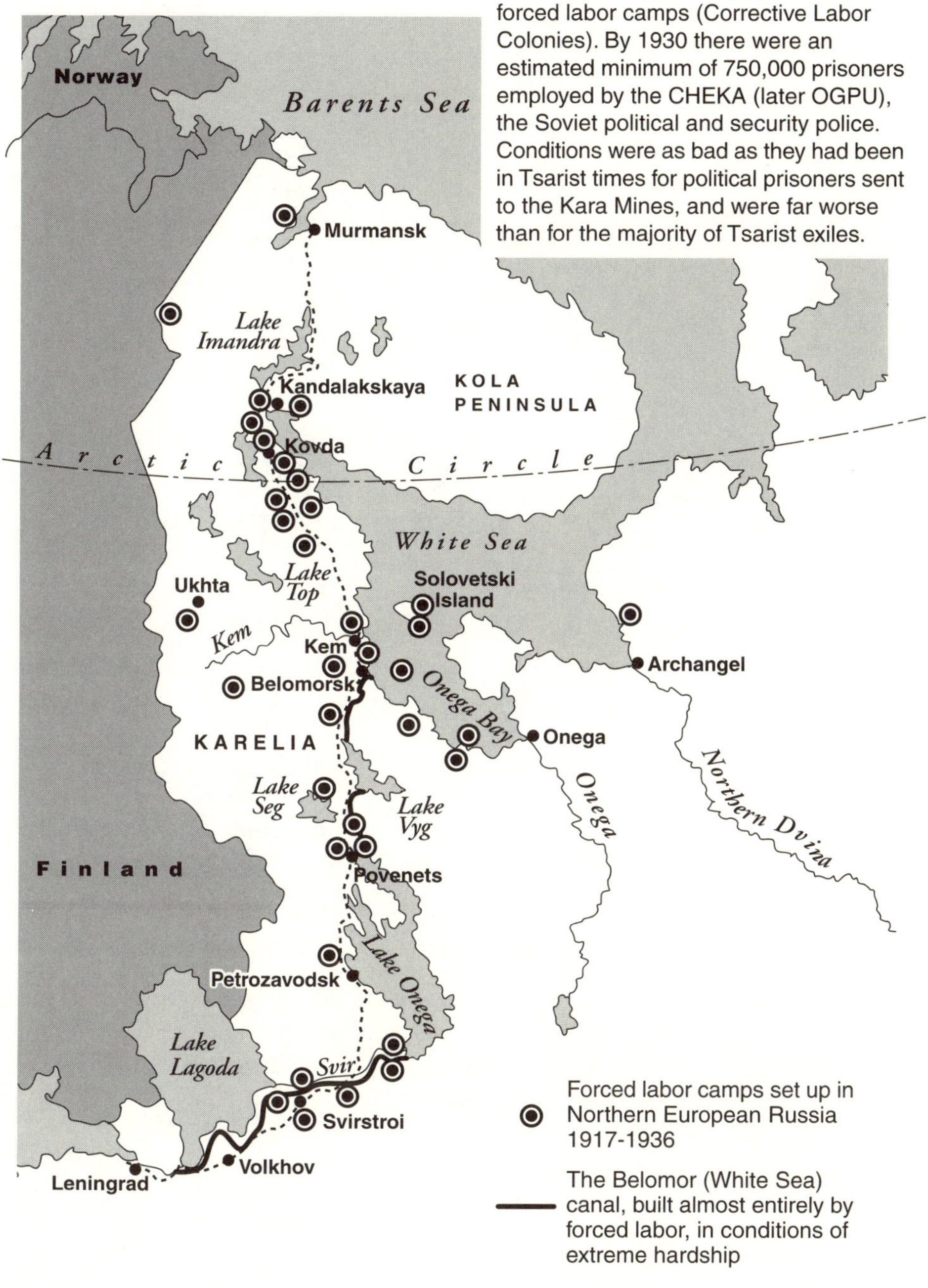

5 Albums.

On August 4, 1992 one of Russia's major newspapers "Izvestia" carried an article with a pun in the title, "The NKVD did the shooting, the Security Ministry of the Russian Federation—the rehabilitating." The ridicule lies in the fact that the organ is the same but the functions—diametrically opposite; the NKVD carried out large-scale punitive measures, while present-day security organs have their hands full doing the clean-up.

Even Russians are often confused on reading different names of one and the same body. Probably a little explaining would help the American reader.

With the advent of Soviet power the CHEKA, later renamed OGPU (the state secret police), headed by "iron Felix," that is Dzerzhinsky, became the all-mighty governing force of the state. Much has been written of its "achievements" in instilling ruthless order. Later this same body was renamed: it became the NKVD (the People's Commissariat of Internal Affairs). In no way should this be interpreted as a narrowing or mitigation of punitive functions, vice versa the scale of terror increased multi-fold. Later all the central organs responsible for leading various branches of national economy were renamed and became People's Commissariats. The intention was to emphasize the role the people of the nation was playing in government maintenance and control (nonsense!). Thus Russia had a number of People's Commissariats—of external affairs, of finances, of agriculture, of heavy industry, of light industry, etc. The bloody trail the NKVD left in its wake was pronounced anti-popular, anti-communist, anti-Marxist, anti-Leninist, anti-party and "anti" whatever. Thus the unlimited power possessed by the NKVD was officially denounced, turned over to party organs, underlining the need to exert party control over punitive organs in order to exclude terror in the policy of the state. (What a display of pharisaism!). People's Commissariats became Ministries, like in the West. Thus two organs appeared instead of one NKVD—the KGB (the State Security Council) and the MVD (the Ministry of Internal Affairs). Many readers are undoubtedly acquainted with "KGB"[13], so there's no need to dwell on the role it played in Soviet society. It was later renamed once again and became the MGB (Ministry of State Security). Today the FSK (Federal Security Service) has replaced the KGB (MGB). This latter renaming, to my mind, reflects the process of democratization that is slowly underway in the country.

So, speaking of the large-scale repressions the Soviet nation was subjected to, we refer to the OGPU and NKVD which are accountable for the tragedies of millions. The rehabilitation process began under the MGB and further—the KGB. Today the FSK is in charge and it was under its wing that I was working in the NKVDA in Petrozavodsk.

"The Grey House" in Petrozavodsk was built in pre-war years and it housed the same offices (excluding the earlier OGPU) and people, but for those who shared the fate of their victims, or the retired. People's Commissars (Narkoms) of Internal Affairs Tenison and Matuzenko excelled in signing death sentences with one bold stroke of the pen. I'm talking about Karelia, which followed the pattern of the center where the Narkoms were replaced in the same manner: Yagoda–Yezhov–Beria: the butchers-in-chief shared the fate of their victims.

Once on coming out of the FSK building after a hard day's job I bumped into a friend. He was rendered speechless on my answer to his question:

"What were you doing there?"

"I work there."

Yes, GPU, NKVD, MGB, KGB evoke sad memories and fear still reigns in the hearts of people! We can only hope that in future FSK will cause no more concern in Russian citizens than CIA does in Americans. Working there should just be doing a job, isn't that so? At least I haven't got a word to say against the way I was treated there throughout my research although I wasn't given ALL the necessary papers regardless of additional written inquiries. Still I can't lay the blame on the individuals who were responsible for supplying me with materials. Naturally, I had to sign separately for each one. An interesting detail. One day when I was waiting for my officer on the visitors' side of the barrier at the FSK an official, whom I happened to know quite well, entered. He greeted me affably, saying they'd find a place for me to work in one of the offices. He was amused to hear my response, "Thank you! I feel safer on THIS side."

The above-mentioned "Izvestia" article cites the words of MGB major-general Anatoly Krayushkin, which, as far as I managed to discover, is the first-ever answer to the question, "What is the total number of Stalinist victims?"

In 1917–1990 "3,853,900 people were convicted in the USSR for treason and similar crimes provided for by other articles of the Criminal Code. 827,995 were sentenced to be shot."

The data for 1930–1953 in Karelia was the following: about 20,000 purge victims; 11,000 of the total were victimized in 1937–1938.

Today it's evident that neither on a country-wide scale, nor on the scale of Republic Karelia are these figures exhaustive. They keep rising and today outstanding scientists talk about 20 million purge victims in the country. The final figure for Karelia hasn't been defined either, but it is also on the rise and only combined efforts of numerous researchers can give the answer. Naturally these same efforts have to be applied in every republic, region and district of the land to get the true total from the bottom up to the top. This remains a huge time-and effort-consuming job.

My immediate task is more modest—to define the names and number of Finnish-Americans victimized in years of Stalinism. As I've already mentioned, my figures have also increased substantially due to archive findings.

Talk of a planned national economy! The regime boasted of the seven-league strides the country was making due to government-owned property and strict planning. Little is known about the fact that the genocide launched by Stalin and his hangmen in the twenties and thirties was also a part of the great plan. In the political sciences course we took in higher education there figured a sinister figure—an economist from Great Britain, Thomas Malthus, who considered wars inevitable as the world populace had to be systematically regulated, i.e. diminished, to guarantee the possibility to feed it. The name of Malthus sent tremors through your body. Just think. Some crazy "bourgeois philosopher" laid the basis to justify the slaughter of millions of innocent people! Never did it occur to the Soviets how this misanthropic philosophy was adopted and perfected by the great leaders Lenin and Stalin, who saw no purpose in waiting for wars. "Class struggle" and "counter-revolutionary bourgeois nationalist organizations" had to be wiped out to ensure the safety of the regime, to find cheap labor to build canals, power stations, railroads and factories.

Exactly how the party organs were involved in the planned butchery is easily traceable today. The 1937 February-March plenary session of the All-Union Communist Party (bolsheviks), (VKP/b/) which, by the way, was discussing reorganization of party activities, actually heralded in a new stage in the state's policy of repressions. The resolutions of this session were enhanced by a resolution of the CC Politbureau on July 2, 1937. The latter served as the final basis for Narkom Yezhov to sign his fatal order of the day N 00447 "On repressive operations against kulaks, criminals and other anti-Soviet elements." This paper was signed on July 30, 1937. The paper elaborated all the details of operations, confirmed the personal make-up of republican and regional non-juridical organs—the "troikas" (a group of three people). The troikas were empowered to exercise justice, conduct interrogation and put sentences into effect. Order 00447 established a quota of arrests for every separate administrative territory, even the number of those to be sentenced to death or imprisonment. This order provided for the arrests of 268,950 men and women; 75,950 of them were to be shot. The control figures for Karelia were 1000, out of which 300 (i.e. 33,3%) were to be shot. There's a good Russian proverb, "Appetit poyavlyaetsa vo vremya yedy"—Eating whets the appetite! These figures proved to be all together too small for local authorities and the Kremlin was bombarded with coded messages to increase the numbers. Once again it was the Politbureau of the Central Committee that stepped in to appease these appetites (January 31, 1938). This paper is important also from the standpoint that among the national NKVD operations the Finns are given prominence. Future events go to prove that local appetites were more than appeased.

Now wasn't Karelia an ideal place to root out the enemy that had penetrated into the fields and forests, the construction sites and plants of Karelia from Finland, Canada and the United States of America? What brought them from civilized parts of the world to this God-forsaken land where they didn't even have proper roofs over their heads? Only the desire to kill honest Soviet people and destroy the very foundation of socialism and world communism.

Developing anti-Finnish sententions became the official policy of party, state and security organizations. One of them was the so-called 1935 party purges. Orders were to pay special attention to foreigners, especially those who had formerly belonged to communist or social-democratic parties of the West; to whether they had or didn't have official party transfers from the country of departure. The border-hoppers, who had always suffered, were most hard hit this time too. A failure to pass this purge was meaningful: some expelled party members were arrested without delay; those who were criticized or received severe reprimands were arrested in the close future or they appeared to be among the first victims when the mass purges were launched.

Before tackling the NKVD files I already had my own index, the lists from "Carelia" with 3,487 names (148—women, 1,847—Finns) of victims rehabilitated after January 16, 1989, in keeping with a decision of the Presidium of the Supreme Soviet of the USSR "Additional measures on rehabilitating victims of repressions in 1930–1940 and the early fifties." I wasn't the only one who had turned to authorities for the rehabilitation of kin before January 16, 1989. Thus Father's name is not among those published in the journal.

So the first two questions (many more were to surface after studying the papers) that confronted me were:

How many of the 1,847 Finns had arrived from the US and Canada?

Who are the victims, who, like Oscar Corgan, had been rehabilitated earlier; what is their number?

Naturally I was apprehensive as to the possibilities of finding exact answers but on getting access to the NKVDA hopes were high.

I was in for surprises all along.

What would the reader associate with the word "album"? A family album? A picture album? A post-card album?

You'll understand my feelings when these hard-cover red albums handed over to me, a few at a time, 38 all in all, turned out to be albums documenting arrests. These albums contained half-page copies of a sentence passed on this or that person. Yes, half a page! (compare notorious crime hearings, involving hundreds of volumes!). The "crimes" are enumerated as absolute facts; a very, very short summary is given of the person himself. Then - the sentence: first or second category. The first category presumed a death sentence, the second—a prison term. These two measures of punishment were also established in Narkom Yezhov's cited order.

In the albums the number of second category sentences is minimal, sometimes—none. (Remember? They were to make up over two thirds?) This is hard to understand when in civilized countries the death penalty has been and remains a serious issue. Further I'll bring forward examples and you'll see what "crimes" a person paid for with his life.

No presumption of innocence, no benefit of doubt, no detailed report of investigation, no proof, no trial! On reading the last line in some papers, "X. admitted himself guilty of the crime/s/ he /she is charged with," I recalled an old friend of mine from Petrozavodsk, Vilho Leino.

Vilho was among the first to be arrested. He returned after six months with lips tightly sealed. I kept pestering him to tell me the story. No way! But one evening, when we were actually celebrating the departure of Vilho and family home to Finland, he rendered his fearful experience. Of course, I had to give a vow of silence, but I dare break it now as he is gone, almost 50 years have passed since then and the truth is coming out.

Every night for over a week running Vilho was taken from his cell for interrogation. Each time, after cruel beatings for his refusal to agree with the charges, he was dragged back to the cell and given no chance to sleep throughout the day. One day, when he was being led along the corridor for the current interrogation, he felt a paper shoved into his fist by another prison inmate being returned to his cell. The note read, "If you want to live, sign a confession." "Well," thought Vilho, "this doesn't seem to be a matter of choice, why not try?" So, upon entering the interrogator's office, he just asked for a paper to sign acknowledging his guilt. Having done it, he got a pat on the back and after a few days of normal sleep and food he got out. Logical? Not at all. But his case is not the only one known. Thus on reading "...agreed with charges" in the albums I envisaged what the person had gone through, although, very few had the same good fortune that had come Vilho's way. They were shot!

Back to the Albums. The death sentence was signed by two—the Narkom and the regional prosecutor. Arrested by a troika, sentenced by a "dvoika" (a group of two)! Such was the "justice" NKVD prisoners got!

Album N 1 refers to December, 1937. 100 victims. All sentenced Category 1. The Album opens with Narkom Tenison's letter to the central NKVD entitled "On liquidating espionage-diversive nationalist organizations and groups in Kondopoga, Pryazha, Tunkua and Pudozh districts." It just has to be translated, as it illustrates points dwelt upon earlier:

"We haven't considered more than 200 cases connected with Finns and we're working on 150 at present. About 500 Finns have been arrested since the operation has been underway. Why haven't we done more along the lines of the Finnish operation? 1. For four months we have been occupied with the Karelian and Russian insurgent operation. We have liquidated a number of organizations that were in existence for a good ten years. This counter-revolutionary basis had to be destroyed! The operation was conducted quite successfully: out of the quota 2,700 the troika has considered 1,600 cases. 2. We were waiting to get similar instructions as to operations connected with the Poles (beyond the quota). That is why I didn't want to exceed the quota at the expense of the Finns. It turns out that fulfilling the quota on Finns has dragged out. In conformity with your request to forward name lists I'm doing that and requesting an extension on the Finnish operation for about a month. With Communist greetings. Tenison".

Album N 5 also opens with a letter signed by Tenison. "Today I'm dispatching Album N 5. Thus by this time we have WORKED OUT (underlining mine.—M.S.) 500 Finns. At present we are working at 200 others. In this operation we have liquidated a number of diversive groups, which were actively engaged in preparing arsons at sawmills, the Kondopoga paper and pulp mill, explosions on sections of the Kirovsky railway, at logger camps, the Onega tractor plant, the Karelavto and communication centers.

Informing you about the results of our efforts in the Finnish operation, I request that you speed up the examination of materials I've already forwarded, as the situation in our prisons has become unbearable (e.g. in Kem the quota is exceeded four-fold, the situation in Petrozavodsk is the same)."

Album N 13. Letter signed by Narkom Tenison, dated January 31, 1938. "We were to present the lists (albums) of materials on the Finnish operation by January 10, 1938. By that time we had already dispatched 12 albums with 1,213 names.

Then we proceeded with preparing the paper work for trials. Later we were again allowed to limit ourselves to albums. In agreement with these orders we are sending you the current album (N 13) with 100 names."

Beginning with Album N 28 there's the signature of a new "Narkom"—Matuzenko who even surpassed his predecessor: 14 people sentenced Category 2 lost their chances for "life" as Matuzenko substituted prison terms for execution.

I have already mentioned that the Albums gave a partial answer to the question, whether the arrested had arrived to Russia from Finland or

America. If in the information about a definite person, you could read "from Canada" "or from "America," which usually implied the USA, and additional confirming evidence was found in the passenger lists or other documents, such a person was from the start defined as a US or Canadian emigrant. Besides those people, I've established the identity of 92 others as Finnish-Americans. But there is one US-born border-hopper—Sulo Minkinen, b.1906, who actually left for Finland in the twenties with his father and crossed the border illegally. Taking his place of birth into consideration, I consider him American.

An essential question would be, "What were these men and women accused of?" There's no way to quote all the charges. It goes without saying that most accusations are tied down to the occupation of a person to make it sound more natural. But some are outwardly idiotic and they can be accounted for only by the imagination of the person who was making up the charge. Soviet Karelia and the country as a whole would have been doomed, even if a small number of charges could stand the test of examination—espionage, arsons, intended demolition of roads, railways and bridges, the undermining of production, intellectual diversions, collecting and handing over to enemy agencies hush-hush information (the deployment and number of troops on Karelian territory, the production volume of enterprises), preparation for overthrowing the Soviet government, anti-Soviet pro-bourgeois propaganda, etc.,etc. Still, just to give the reader an idea of these nonsensical charges, I'll quote a few:

HUUKI Kalle, b.US, Mexico—(?), 1898, lived in Finland. "There Huuki fell under the influence of Finland's intelligence service and was packed off to America, where he continued working in its favor. In 1931 shipped to Russia with a special mission."

NORLUND Viktor. Agronomist by education. "Ruined crop rotation in the Kalevala district by intentionally plowing hay fields and thus destroying the collective farm's fodder crops."

KOPPOLA Viktor. "Classified valuable construction timber as third-rate; discredited the Stakhanov movement in talks with workers, promoted slack labor discipline."

KOSKELAINEN Alexander. "While working at the Ilyinsky sawmill ruined the driving belt and thus put the sawmill out of operation for 15 days." "In 1934 as shop steward at the Karelavto intentionally disrupted the transportation plan, which led to a 30–35% exploitation of transport, and distant rural districts were left without food staples."

AALTONEN Maunu. “In 1928 was sent by Finland’s intelligence service to Canada with the purpose a) to leave for Karelia; b) to establish contact with Finland’s agent Karjalainen there and get a concrete espionage assignment. In 1935 contacted an espionage-diversive group in Matrosa, Karelian ASSR, where he burned down 3 hectares of forest.”

KYTOMAKI Kalle. “In 1925 recruited by the Finnish Intelligence Service in Vyborg. Received two assignments: 1) to leave for Canada and recruit people for Karelia; 2) upon arriving in Russia to establish contact with Finland’s Leningrad consul and send information to him in future. Kytomaki reported on the number of Finns in Matrosa. In 1937 he burned down 200 square meters of lumber and 20 hectares of forest.”

HILL Helen. “Maintained contacts with relatives in the US. Collected information in favor of Finland’s intelligence service. Praised life in capitalist countries. Spoke of her intentions to cross the border creating a spirit of emigration in the workers.”

KARHINEN Hanna. “In 1918 arrived in Russia illegally from Finland. The same year was sent to the US by the Communist party of Finland. In the US recruited by Finnish agent Martines. Lived in Seattle. Before departing for Russia in 1926 received assignment from Martines to establish contacts with Finland’s agent Usenius (arrested) in Petrozavodsk.”

MERILÄ Alfred. “Recruited in US by Tenhunen. Established contact with agent Ida R., to whom he passed on information about supplying Petrozavodsk with electric power and its power resources. In preparation for a diversive act at a power station he discovered all its weak spots in advance.” (Merilä was a symphony orchestra musician!)

TAMMINEN Toivo. “His wife left for Finland. He has a house of his own.”

MÄKI Oscar. “From Finland to America in 1911. Went in for trade. Had his own sawmill with up to 20 workers. In 1932 went bankrupt and decided to go to Russia. Recruited by Latva in Toronto.”

FINBERG Väinö. “Increased the publication of counter-revolutionary nationalist literature by cutting down Russian and Karelian language publications.”

MÄKI Jaakko. “Made incisions in new car tires. As a result the plan for transporting logs was disrupted.”

BIRCH Emil. “Intentionally created national rife by granting Finns better working conditions. Made the drawings of and built a 1500 kwt feeder station at the Solomennoye power station instead of the required

3000 kwt.".

KULMALA Arvik. "Working as a stableman in Uhtua, intentionally distributed the harness wrong: bigger horses got smaller harness which caused sores from rubbing. Didn't have the manes cut in order to harm the horses' range of visibility."

HALLIKAINEN Henrik. "Sent to Canada in 1930 by the Finnish Intelligence Service, where he underwent a 6-month course in espionage training and received a 10 thousand FM remuneration. In 1933 sent to Karelia, where he settled down for espionage at the Kondopoga paper and pulp mill. In 1937 became a secret NKVD agent."

Approaching the last score of albums I found my chums - all gifted musicians, United States born lads aged 19 at the time they were torn from their parents. I had to make apologies for the tell-tale tear stains left on the pages.

TUOMELA Keijo. "Recruited by intelligence agent Olavi Siikki. (siikki had already been arrested by that time himself)." "Tuomela collected information on the number of troops deployed in Petrozavodsk, on educational work in the schools and university of Petrozavodsk, on military orders received by enterprises, the number of workers employed and the production capacity of enterprises."

MÄKELA Kalervo. "A terrorist-spy. Collected and passed on to Pushko (the name is not familiar) espionage information on the population's sentiments, on ski factory productivity, on the construction of the town's railway station."

SWORD Ansa. "Recruited by Nyström; took pictures of industrial enterprises: the Onega plant, the ski factory, the airport, military warehouses, power stations, the city bakery, the NKVD building, collected information on the deployment of troops in Petrozavodsk, their armament." (never had we seen Ansa with a camera. They were rarities in those days.)

KAUPPI Theodore and RANTALA Olavi were charged with espionage of the same character. Only Olavi, or Liver, as we called him, was 21! He returned. I could find no document confirming his acquittal.

Reading these names and the insinuations attached to them I kept turning the pages, calling back the images of these handsome young lads and found what I was looking for on the very distant shelves of stored memories.

1938. The eve of May Day celebrations. We liked partying but this time, for some reason or other, we decided to have a big blow-out, getting together as large a crowd of peers as possible. Today two of us remain, a third might still be on this side of time, but I couldn't locate her in Finland where she had moved. Thus Vieno and I put our heads together reminiscing on details of the last happy hours some 20 of us had spent together.

Remember my description of the houses the Finnish-Americans put up in Petrozavodsk, the so-called Valiparakit?. Eight rooms on one landing, one common kitchen, wood-stoves and a clothes closet in every room? We chose one of these houses for the party as families with three of our girls (the Honka sisters Inga and Sirkka, Aileen Sarkkinen), the Mäkeläs with Kalervo, rather Cowboy, as he was called, and Rudy had rooms here. The eldest Mäkelä brother Reino had a room of his own on the same landing and he was always willing to support us kids. They talked it up with the neighbors and we were given a free hand up to 12 p.m.: use the kitchen, dance in the corridor, smoking on the stairwell only! Have a good but orderly time!

One room was the "Jokes only." That's where Reino Mäkelä, Ansa Sword and Ensio Haapanen reigned. It was non-stop joking: one got through, laughter hadn't yet subsided when the next one took over. A second room was for games. A third—for hors d'oeuvres and beer (naturally, some guys had pocket flasks too. You couldn't exactly picture Russia without them!). The fourth was for coffee, tea and the goodies made by the girls. And in the corridor—dancing to grammaphone music (some of the melodies still ring in my ears!). It happened that somebody would accidentally stumble on a couple kissing and hugging in the kitchen, or on the stairs that led to the attic or in a neglected corner. A girlish tear was shed here and there. You know how it is: A is in love with B, while B is in love with C etc. That was happening all along. The fun was at its height when neighbors started returning, so the party began breaking up and the boys went to see off the girls.

That party was a gift of fate. It was the last time we were all together, enjoying ourselves to the full. Whoever bumped into a pal who had been at the party had a lot to talk about. But soon the fun was cut short and replaced by fear, anger and sorrow: we began losing the boys one by one. Never did it occur to the families or to us, the friends, that we'd never see them again. Never did it occur to me that there'd come a day when I'd be involved in trying to do my bit in restoring the honor and very names of these American lads and that I'd find them in "Albums" bearing witness to the incomprehensible destruction of innocent lives. Believe it or not, but when I learned that their sentences had been put into effect in September the same year, I was relieved to realize that they didn't have to go through the unbearable torture of camps. The names of Cowboy and Ansa stand in the same execution list, so probably they even had the "luck" to support each other, to be together to the last! We have aged, but they'll never grow old! Blond, over six-feet tall Keijo with his clarinet. Not at all Finnish-looking darkish Cowboy with his French horn. Brown-eyed handsome Ansa with his trombone. Shortish, sturdily built Teddy with his trumpet. Maybe they were thus inhumanely spared the privations of wars and labor camps that became the fate of their peers? This is a poor consolation, indeed!

These same Albums served as a source of information disconnected with the fates of Finnish-Americans, but oh, how revealing of the times, of the tragedies that had become the lot of the nation as a whole.

Only in the period of the temporary Khrushchev "thaw" did we begin hearing about the repressions the rural population had been subjected to. We heard talk about whole villages being wiped out, about deaths of millions due to famine. But having no local information it seemed far-off and detached, although the varied crimes of the regime left no doubt. The figures were staggering and, as it turned out, Karelia hadn't been spared either.

My People perished in the NKVD so-called Finnish operation. But a closer examination of each Album shows that not only Finns were included, e.g.

	Finnish-Americans	from Finland	others
Album N4	4	41	55
Album N5	17	45	38
Album N8	18	31	51
Album N13	20	38	42
Album N14	28	40	32 etc.

It's evident that in Karelia the number of immigrant victims from Finland outweighs all others, as does the number of emigrants from Finland, as compared to those who arrived from northern America. But who are "the others"? Although some of them bear Russian-style family names, they are Karelians—people belonging to the same Fenno-Ugrian race we do.

Since my search was tied down to a definite category of people, at first I kind of disregarded other names. But when one and the same name began appearing again and again, I had to take a better look. There was no turning back to Albums I had already gone through, but the names of Fofanovs and Larionovs from Tunkua, of Koshkins and Semyonovs from the village of Buldyry, the Louhi district, Semyonovs and Yeliseyevs from the Rugozero district kept cropping up. Thus, when I came across the first seven Languyevs in Album N 21, I was on the alert. Fathers and sons: Languyev Ivan (1887) and sons Herman (1911) and Ivan (1908); Languyev Mikhail (1875) and sons Trofim (1910) and Larion (1914), Languyev Pavel (1888). Album 22—Languyev Filip (1908); Album N 24 Languyev Daniil (1904), Languyev Nikolai (1900). All from the present-day non-existent village of Tikshozero, the Kies-tin-ki district. All with wives and children (there were five children in the family of Nikolai Languyev). Now what could they have been accused of? Here's an example:

Languyev Pavel. Illiterate (the fact is recorded), was charged with working under the guidance of a Finland resident Victor Hill (from the US) since 1936. The latter, by the way, lived in Uhtua and the only way of sending information would have been in writing by pigeon post. Languyev supplied the "resident" with information about the deployment of border guard troops.

In Finland's military archives I discovered the name of a young prisoner of war Mikko Languyev, b.1920, who had escaped to Sweden. It's beyond doubt that he belongs to the same family and it's not hard to understand why he lengthened the distance between himself and his native land. I hope he made good!

Before closing the final page on "Albums" (1937–1938) there's another observation I'd like to share with my reader: the frequent use of the term "concentration camp". Ask any native of Russia where and when this word originated. You're sure to hear: "In Hitler Germany. That's where the fascists held, tortured and killed POWs." It's really up to linguists now to establish who, when and under what circumstances was the first to come up with this term the mere mentioning of which was for years to instill horror in people all over the world!

6 Protocols.

Now this, I thought, is where I'll find the final answers to all questions pertaining to the disappearances of hundreds of Finnish-Americans. This, I thought, is where I'll find the final answer to the question, "How many people were murdered in Karelia or sentenced to spend the rest of their days in gulags?" I also expected to discover where the mass graves of innocent victims could be found in the republic. But my hopes were dashed to the ground. Once more was I convinced that there was only one way to find these answers, that is by making thorough case studies of one and each file.

There's very little to be said about the location of mass graves. Nobody knows, nor, as a matter of fact, will ever know. You can get an idea of where the shootings happened only judging by the addressees to whom lists of those sentenced were dispatched for the sentence to be put into effect: it sometimes happened that the name of the NKVD district department was mistakenly indicated.

So where could we stick in a pin to mark mass graves on the graveland map of Karelia? Here:

Petrozavodsk (Petroskoi), numerous outskirts of the city, like Bessovets, Sulazhgora, Kamenny Bor;

Olonets (Aunus);

Kem (Kemi);

Rugozero (Rukajärvi);

Pudozh;

Kandalaksha (Kantalahti, Murmansk region; at the time of the mass arrests was a part of Karelia);

Kondopoga; (Kontupohja);

Belaya Gora, Kondopoga;

Territory of roadside leading to Poduzhem (Kem district);

400–450 meters to the side of the road leading to Uhtua (it's "only" 183 meters long!);

Medvezhyegorsk (Karhumäki), BBK NKVD management;

Medvezhyegorsk.

Reburials of remains have taken place in Pudozh and Petrozavodsk. The Karelian newspapers have described serious attempts to discover the graves in other places, including Medvezhyegorsk, where my father was shot. They have all been in vain: as a rule, the executors met with the same fate as their victims. Without doubt that was also the lot of Kem NKVD driver Potyokhin whose written pledge of silence was not extracted from the papers by mistake (it's the only one of its kind!). It's written in pencil: "I vow not to disclose the fact of shooting eight people off the road leading to Poduzhem. August 11, 1937. Potyokhin." This date is incompatible with that of protocol N 1, which also gives reason to believe that not all the shootings are reflected in documents.

The protocols under consideration date from September 20, 1937 (N 1), to October 10, 1938 (N 32). These documents are signed by the Extraordinary Troika made up of the Narkom of the republic (Tenison or Matuzenko), the First Secretary of the Regional Party Committee (Kupriyanov) and Chief Prosecutor (Mikhailovich). The fate of the Narkoms has already been mentioned. Kupriyanov remained in the office of chief Karelian party boss up to the post war years when he was transferred to Leningrad. There he was arrested in connection with the so-called Leningrad Party case. After Stalin's death this fabricated case was crushed, he and family (wife was also arrested, children packed off to NKVD children's homes) survived, although many others, involved in the Leningrad case, were done away with. I just wonder whether these 32 lengthy bloody documents Kupriyanov signed ever came to mind when he was pacing the walls of his own cell, pondering on the righteous course of his life or writing appeals demanding justice. His appeals were heard and satisfied, but not those of the 1937–1938 victims!

The protocols reflect the nationalistic policy pursued in the republic, although being a Russian didn't save one from persecution either. There was not only a Finnish operation, but a German, Polish, Latvian, British, Estonian, Swedish, French and Japanese as well. They didn't involve great numbers of "criminals," sometimes only one as in the case of Vasili Bogdanov from the fishing village of Shuyeretskoye on the White Sea. Having served in Miller's army (British occupational forces in the Civil War) he escaped to London when the Red Army took over. Thinking everything had quieted down he returned to his native parts in 1920 (the date can be subjected to doubt) and went back to fishing. But he was reminded of his "betrayal" in 1937 when they came and picked him up as a British spy. Who knows, he might have been counting the cod, halibut, plaice and white fish and passing the information on to the M-5!

Working on the albums and protocols was a devastating task: the numbers were crushing, the sentences horrendous. Your imagination drew the rest. But reading what you did was what set the mind working. A few examples:

The waves of arrests were so swift and merciless that even the obedient executors of inhuman orders coming from the top were at a loss. A letter from chief of the Kandalaksha district NKVD to KASSR NKVD head Tenison, dated October 12, 1937: "We have 199 prisoners. Our space provides for 50. In order to alleviate the circumstances we are turning to you with the following requests: allow us to send to Petrozavodsk the 48 inmates whose cases are already in the hands of the troika (presumably, he's talking about the Big or Extraordinary troika!). This would enable us to cut the number down to 120–130 ***units*** (no mistake in the translation!) and go on liquidating counter-revolutionary insurgents with greater speed: we already have evidence against 70–80.

Besides, we consider it our duty to inform you that putting sentences into effect is becoming more and more difficult under the circumstances.

If up to now, when the number of arrested was smaller and we managed to keep everything in secret from the population and other criminals, it'll be much more complicated in future, as the preliminary ***work-out*** (no mistake in the translation!) has to be done in our offices, which means there's no way to go on with investigations in the building.

Dealing with 3–4 units would be easier, while dealing with 20–30 causes excesses pending exposure. The department is located in the center of the settlement in its busiest and best lighted place, as you know.

And yet worse, if all this reaches the ears of those who are behind prison walls, it'll make it impossible to withdraw 20 units without attracting attention. It could lead to escape attempts or attacks on the innumerous convoy."

Besides linguistic improperties and indirect allusion to manhandling, there's another point which I tried, but to no avail, lucidate in the NKVDA. I'm sure the reader will draw the same conclusion as I did: not every arrested passed the Big Troika: they were shot on the spot at the responsibility of the local NKVD. So wouldn't that mean that their names are not registered in the Albums and Protocols under observation? I have reason to express this opinion as pure arithmetical calculations don't even live up to the minimum of illegally arrested, expressed earlier—11,000 victims in 1937–1950. Where are the other names?

My mentioning earlier that Soviets took the abbreviation BBK for "gulag" was not for nothing. Here's a little proof of what went on even after the canal was built. BBK remained faithful to its name. Chief of department 3, BBK NKVD Astrov received papers and orders to execute 400 arrested. This killing occurred from November 28, 1937, to December 15, 1937. In 19 days 400 executions! The shooting was at its height on December 9, when 119 innocent men got a bullet in the back of their heads.

The protocols abound in inconsistencies.

Protocol N 2, September 20, 1938, reads, "Hand over to convoy chief Bolshakov the following 62 arrested (out of 100) to be accompanied "na etap."(in Russian these two words refer to a place/places along the road to the final gulag). Among these 62 names there are 28 arrivals from America who, as you'll discover in appendix N 1, were rehabilitated, showing the year of their death as 1938, which speaks for itself: Emil Koskela, Hilda Kauppi, Helen-Melise Kallila, Sakari Kankaanpaa, Leo Kuula, Kustaa Koivisto, Albert Marttila, Urho Santti, Henrik Hill, Juho Juvonen, Toivo Saari.

The names of 16 others are not in rehabilitation lists. They are included in appendix N 3. But seeing that the eleven above-mentioned were actually exterminated, doesn't it give reason to presume that all 62 prisoners met with the same fate—execution? The bookkeeping, as you see, isn't properly balanced. So this gives ample reason to consider that all these "documents" cannot be accepted at face value.

Thus once again we come to the same conclusion: the answer could be found only in the victim's personal file!

Similar examples are to found in other protocols as well and I attach special importance to this fact as it goes to prove that the number of those shot drastically exceeds the number of those who were packed off to gulags to suffer and, in most cases, to die.

One of the particularities of the Russian grammar system is the gender: in the past tense the ending Λ–stands for the masculine, the Λa–for the feminine. In addressing a grown-up or speaking of him the patronymic is used: Nina Ivanovna or Nikolai Ivanovich, Maria Petrovna or Vladimir Petrovich. Honor Thy Father! Either the NKVD officials' grammar was poor or they didn't know whether they were dealing with a man or a woman. It really didn't make any difference to them! I've discovered many examples of the kind, here's one. In the same Protocol N 2 Helen-Melise Kallila (people who knew her claim she was a beauty) figures as a man. Opposite her name we read, in the masculine, of course, "this prisoner has already been shot!"

On reading that Arthur Alanko had died of a natural cause (the same goes for William Tolonen, Onni Alt, Uuno Lappalainen) you cannot but read another meaning into this information!

Now who were the executioners? How many were there? What were the feelings they experienced at these mass exterminations that were going on simultaneously in many places?

You may agree with me or you may not. But with criminality running riot in Russia today I find a direct connection between the crimes of the past and those of today. The misanthropic philosophy denying human rights, disacknowledging the significance and uniqueness of one life has laid the basis for terror and impunity. Just as the criminals who perpetuated the butchery of the thirties were never brought to trial, the guilty ones are going stock free today, or is this becoming a genetic problem? Within the past 5–6 years Russians have seen a few hangmen of the thirties in documentaries. They don't acknowledge their guilt, they call themselves obedient servants of the government and claim to have been obeying orders and that's all. They even enjoy government pensions for their "loyalty" and they praise the communist regimes. The most atrocious example would be that of the son of butcher-in-chief Beria. The son has written and published a book whitewashing his father; he even made a TV appearance expounding his ideas. Hitler's "Mein Kampf" has found its reader in present-day Russia. It's not hard to imagine the mentality of the two generations of young people that have grown up in families headed by those who are directly responsible for much of the evil that reigned in the country. It's terrifying!

But now I'll get back to Finnish-Americans where the situation is clearer. How did the regime get away with this gross violation of human rights? Wasn't there danger of the question arising in the West, "What the hell is going on?" Among the arrested there even were foreign citizens (Walter Manners, Eino Eskola—both from the US); family members had returned to America either before or after the "disappearance" of a father, brother, sister or mother; a number of the arrested were known for their loyalty to communist party principles. What if relatives or communist party organs in foreign countries raise a row and begin questioning the legality of arrests in the Soviet Union?

That didn't happen but for a few cases quoted in "Red Exodus". Silence is agreement, so nothing changed. And the silence maintained by the US and Canadian communist party officials was a downright betrayal of their former comrades. Immigrants from America and Finland just kept on disappearing.

There was silence on the European side of the Atlantic too. But this silence was broken in 1939 by Chairman of the Communist International Executive Committee Georgi Dimitrov at whose initiative Gennady Kupriyanov's article "In the forests of Karelia" was published in the April 23, 1939 issue of "Pravda." Judging by the article itself and events that followed, some complaints by Americans had caused a little splash in the Comintern. So Kupriyanov received two basic tasks: first, to prove that there actually had been some (no facts!) counter-revolutionary activity on behalf of Canadians (the US wasn't mentioned) in Karelia in favor of Finland, but the blame was to be laid at the door of the Karelian Technical Aid. Retaliation appeared in the form of closing down the KTA in 1939, when that had already happened long ago: the KTA had not been functioning since 1934. Second, to publish materials in the mass media reflecting the happy productive labor of Canadians in Karelia to prove that complaints were groundless.

Researcher Irja Takala cites a 1938 NKVD paper she discovered in the Karelian party archives which throws light on the number of illegal arrests of immigrants. "All together during the Finnish operation from November, 1937, to April, 1938, we have arrested and exposed as agents of Finnish intelligence agencies and participants of counter-revolutionary organizations:

1.	Border-hoppers	1357
2.	Political emigrants	54
3.	Legal immigrants from Finland to Russia	115
4.	Legal immigrants from Canada and the USA	342
		Total 1868 [14]

On the basis of what you have already read, you are aware that the arrests began much earlier than November, 1937, and were in full swing up to the autumn of 1938. This fact alone suffices to consider the quoted paper unreliable, including the number of Finnish-American Stalinist victims, which you'll find in the afterword.

You'd logically expect to find the names of all Stalinist victims in documents mentioned or considered: the "Albums," "Protocols" and rehabilitation papers: either in "Carelia" or in "Petrozavodsk." But that is not the case.

A survey of these papers has shown:

a) many victims don't figure anywhere. But their victimization leaves no doubt, as the families received rehabilitation papers in the Khrushchev-era. The reader will find their names in appendix 4;

b) not every arrested person had a family, or the family members have given no notice of themselves. Still, since their co-workers remember that they were led away by NKVD agents. The figure 62 is included in the victims.

The compiling of appendix 3 revealed a strange phenomenon: the Protocols contained names of victims who were not to be found in the Albums. These cases have been marked*. But if a person's name was indicated in both "Albums" and "Protocols," only the latter, as the final document, is indicated.

The "Protocols" end with N 32, but they are followed by Archive files bearing other numbers. Since a few Finnish-Americans were found in these lists too, they will be indicated: e.g."P-A-141".

Consequently, the fact that Oscar Corgan's execution on January 9, 1938 was determinable only on the basis of his personal file goes to prove, as illustrated above, that his case is not the only one. To my mind, this can be accounted for by the fact that during the Khrushchev "thaw" relatives appealed directly to Moscow, e.g.Tenhunen's and Corgan's rehabilitation came from Moscow, from the Supreme Court of the USSR.

Still another indestructible barrier remains. Dissatisfied with the Karelian conditions numerous Finnish-Americans and families moved to other parts of the country where they met with the same tragic fate. Their papers, naturally, are not to be found in Karelia. One example. The family of Emil and Maria Rautiainen, whom you'll read about further on, was brutally torn apart in Ukraine. They were rehabilitated but not in Karelia. There's no way to say how many other victims of the kind could be found on the one-sixth of the world then called the USSR.

Anna, Otto, Paula and Kerttu Granholm. Otto is one of the 62 who has not yet been found. Photo courtesy of Kerttu Granholm.

Hopefully the day will come when there'll be a final answer to all the questions. Only never will the kin of these victims have a place to go to remember as it happens all over the United States on Memorial Day, a nationwide holiday when kin and citizens bow their heads in reverence of those who have passed on. A beautiful tradition!

7 Wars.

Never has war brought anything but devastation, misery and grief in its wake. And when you think that it's foremostly the young ones who go, men whose life hasn't even begun, a sense of endless sadness, piercing to the very heart, grows upon you.

To draw the map of Graveland Karelia we'll have to pose the same question, "Where could we pinpoint the mass graves of the wars waged on Karelian territory?" Nobody knows exactly. But we do know that huge military operations were conducted on Karelian territory and that the losses were of great magnitude.

THE WINTER WAR

The English-reading public got some staggering information on the Winter War. Taking into consideration the time factor, the choice of place for attack, the outnumbering Soviet troops, armaments and equipment, military experience Khrushchev admitted, "...even in these most favorable conditions it was only after great difficulty and enormous losses that we were finally able to win. A victory at such a cost was actually a moral defeat."[15] But who in Russia was aware of this estimation? Only the rulers, who made sure that such information did not leak out!

For over 50 years the nation was hoodwinked into believing that little Finland had treacherously attacked Giant Russia. Only in our days has it become evident how Russia had been coveting the territory surrounding

Leningrad and was out to get it by hook or by crook. But since theoretically there was no way a socialist country could attack its neighbor the stage was laid to make it look vice versa. Historical facts came late to the people of Russia and only due to the system of openness that was appearing in Gorbachev's time.

In the late thirties, when the wounds of Poland and the purges were still raw, new tragedies were already in the making. November 1939 saw an incomprehensible concentration of troops in the vicinity of the old state border in Karelia and Leningrad. There was talk about maneuvers. This didn't spell disaster, as maneuvers are maneuvers and every army conducts them from time to time. There was another unexpected eye-opener, and a shattering one at that, but familiar only to music-lovers, strange as it may seem. Late in the autumn of 1939 the Leningrad Military district jazz orchestra under Boris Schmidt visited Petrozavodsk. The concerts were well-attended and to the utter astonishment of the audience the following song was heard:

"We want the Urals,"—
Is what they were shouting,
Militant gangs
In their chants of war.
Oh, but, generals,
You won't see the mountains,
It's over in Helsinki
We want to see you more.

At the same time Finnish and Karelian young men were being drafted into the so-called National Army, the puppet O.W. Kuusinen National Government was formed. It was evident that something was up. The mass media was also doing its bit: now and then news items on insignificant border incidents appeared. Besides, we should bear in mind, that the anti-Finnish language campaign was barely over (1937–1938): the Finnish language had been ousted from school curricula, Finnish publications closed down. Within the past years the press had abounded in information on Finland's agents intercepted and justly punished by state punitive organs. The "foreign threat" policy was the official policy of the state and it kept hammering on this idea in so many direct and indirect ways that the misled people took it for granted. The fact that the populace was from the first days of the revolution brought up in the spirit, "Why think? We're doing it for you" enabled the party, NKVD and the Soviets (the official governmental organs) to manipulate public opinion. This gave the bellicose leaders the green light which led to so many tragedies, including Afghanistan in the seventies and Chechnya in the nineties.

Has the information void disappeared? Have the people of the former Soviet Union learned the truth about the Winter War? My answer would be "No."

In 1994 the 55th anniversary of this inhuman war was given prominence in the Russian mass media and scientific circles. The local Petrozavodsk paper "Severny Kuryer" carried a reprint of a "Moscow News" article by P. Aptekarj. In big letters the title reads, "Blood-covered snow," the subtitle, "This year 55 years have come to pass since the Soviet-Finland war—one of the most ignominious pages in the history of this country. But new archive data make it possible to get a more complete understanding of the course it ran, of what the peoples of the USSR had to pay for the political ambitions of the Soviet leadership. The main conclusion of the 1939–1940 campaign is 130,000 killed and missing." "In April 1940, over 6,000 POWs were handed over to Soviet representatives in Vyborg. 700 badly wounded were hospitalized. The rest were sent to gulags in Norilsk."

June 6-10, 1994, Petrozavodsk University sponsored an international conference "Karelia, Zapolyarye and Finland in the years of World War II." My talk in the discussion was based on materials uncovered in my research. But it was more important for me to ask a question pertaining to the losses of the Soviet side in the Winter War: I was baffled by the one million quoted by Khrushchev in his memoirs, so I decided that the presence of specialists on the topic from the Russian side had to be taken advantage of. This is what we heard from an outstanding scholar on Russia-Finland relations PhD Nikolai Baryshnikov, "I doubt if the exact figure will ever be known." Support came from an unexpected quarter. Prof. Alla Fyodorova from Orenburgh explained that in preparation for this conference their chair had investigated whether there were any families in this far-off Ural region that had lost fathers or sons in the Winter War. The collected information was staggering: from four to six victims in almost every village. "Shouldn't a monument to these senselessly lost lives be put up in every settlement?" she asked.

There is one well-documented book that should be translated into Russian and spread in the country. I'm referring to "The Winter War. The Soviet Attack on Finland" by Eloise Engle and Lauri Paananen".[16] This tribute to the Finnish nation has sure made the round of my English-reading friends.

The adjoining map will make it easier to answer the question about where to mark the Winter War losses. Only the number is vague.

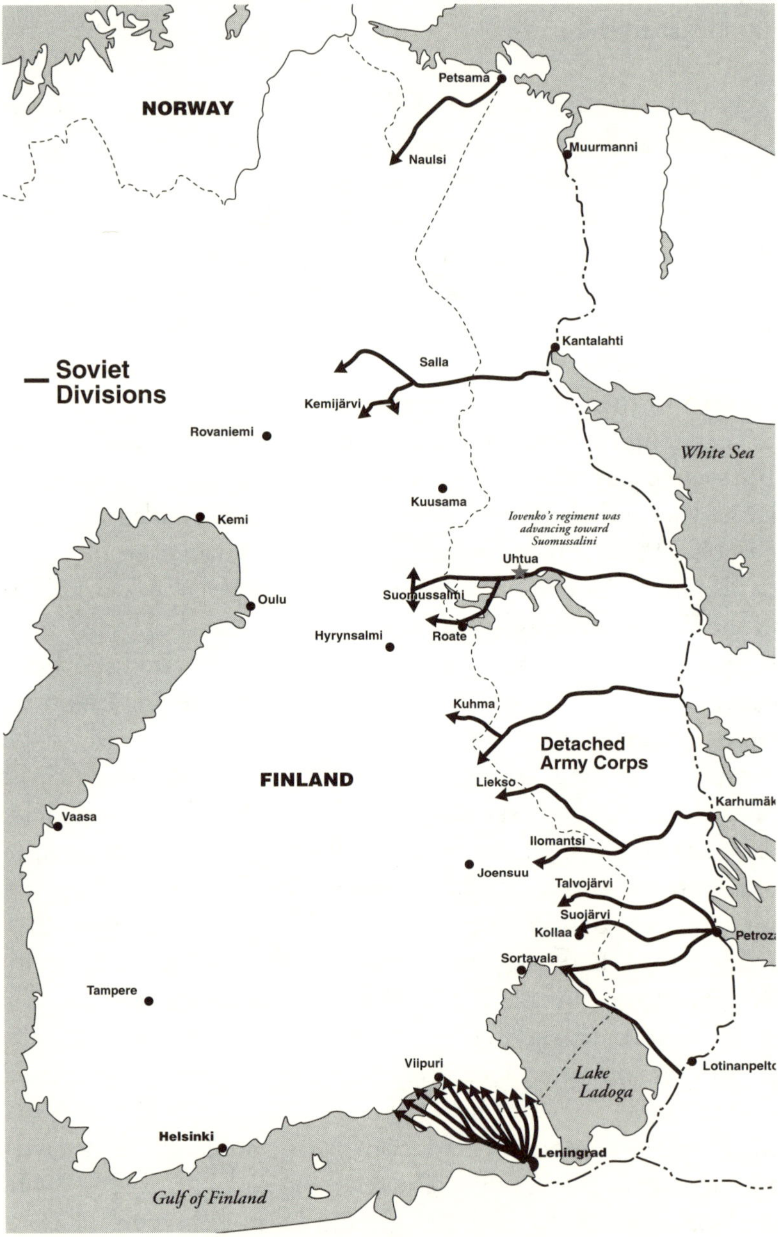

Hopefully a short rendering of another "Severny Kuryer" article "The tragedy not far from Uhtua" (September 9, 1995) will be of help. It's written by a Winter War veteran Alexander Iovenko, living today in Ukraine. An introduction by Petrozavodsk journalist A. Gordienko precedes the story. He writes "The frightening truth of these events is shattering. I hope it will not affect the friendly relations we have with Finns today. But what happened just happened; you can't throw the words out of a song, not even a sad one." Yes, but as I see it, every native of the country should experience a deep sense of shame and pain on reading the story. Shame for the disregard the Soviet State showed (and is showing) for its citizens, pain for the families who lost their menfolk and don't even know where their last resting place is. Here's the tragic incident, which Iovenko claims is but one of many:

In September 1939 the regiment Iovenko was serving in was dispatched to the Polish front. They were in battle for only four days when the new state border was established: the "reunification" of former Ukrainian and Bielorussian territories to the USSR was completed. The regiment returned to Novograd-Volynsk and the troops were counting the days left till demobbing. But they had another guess coming: new weapons and armaments were coming in, elderly men were being drafted to replace losses, young lieutenants, turned out before their time, appeared on the regiment scene.

After a short wait the officers got to know that their regiment was being dispatched to a part of the country without sun but with permafrost. War with Finland was already going on. So it wasn't hard to figure out where they were being sent. The stories they heard about Finnish snipers sitting in tree-tops killing the enemy and the lightning knifings that brought down Russians caused alarm and panic. They had feared the worst and it came to happen.

The regiment was included in a division which was loaded on an Arkhangelsk-bound train. Fears kept rising and with them — self-inflicted wounds: within two months there were 197 of them. The officers got white sheepskin coats and "valenki" (thick felt boots), but the soldiers' equipment was so poor that there already were many cases of frostbites after the 30-kilometer march that finally brought them to the port where "Shchors" was anchored in wait for the division. The heavy equipment was loaded on barges and they set off guided by two icebreakers "Lenin" and "Stalin." (Very symbolic, isn't it?)

Spirits rose when Kandalaksha finally loomed into sight in the frosty mist: the heavy seas had also taken a toll. Regiment 743 with Iovenko was the first to disembark, it was followed by trucks carrying food supplies and ammunition. The medical battalion wound up the two-kilometer long procession. The frost kept intensifying. First snowbanks prevented trucks and heavy equipment from making headway, then motors froze into immobility. Red-blue flames of welding lamps flickered near all the trucks: it was the only way to thaw the motors. After ten-to fifteen kilometer stages there were warm-up stops. The soldiers chopped off fir-tree branches to heat food and water, to cover the icy ground. Moving closer to the fire, hugging one another tightly, they instantaneously fell into a dead slumber. After every 30 minutes a crisp order cut the silence: "Over on the other side!" But for such a measure of precaution the exhausted soldiers would have frozen to death.

Further advance was slow: the heavy equipment was pulled by manual force. It was lifted onto self-made runners and pulled by soldiers and officers harnessed into ropes. Iovenko claims he'll never forget how they finally reached their destination late one night. The dugouts were made and quickly occupied by the soldiers. It was warm there with fires burning in a barrel in the middle, but the stench was unbearable.

The food supplies had dwindled down to nil. All they had was sour cabbage soup (shchi) with frozen deer meat. The soldiers were hungry, freezing to death and ready to fall asleep standing. The frosts kept worsening: it was below 40 degrees C. The officers were called to the headquarter dug-out. Orders were issued to put up guards to ensure the safety of the regiment.

Iovenko fell asleep sitting in the headquarter dugout and he attributes his life to his state of overfatigue.

The enemy had been keeping a close eye on the regiment. It acknowledged the exhausted state of the men. No sooner had the soldiers crawled into their dug-outs and the guards assumed their positions than the Finns swooped down the hills on skis, killed the guards, entered the dug-outs stabbing the sleeping soldiers and machine-gunning those who tried to escape. Iovenko writes it was the first time Russian soldiers had ever seen such machine-guns.

The Finns left as speedily and silently as they had come. The havoc they had caused was hair-raising. Iovenko took charge of registering the killed, saving documents and organizing the burial of the 720 killed. The living made no secret of their tears, their sufferings, their helplessness. Each was asking himself the same questions, "Why did this happen? Who is to blame?"

The final words in his story, "That's how Ukrainian men found their last resting place near a nameless hill not far from Uhtua in the cold Karelian soil."

The map indicates other places, places where the losses were no smaller and probably no less dramatic. The Karelian graveland keeps expanding!

For two poets, one Russian, the other Finnish, Yev. Dolmatovski and Yrjö Jylhä, the best way to impart their shattering Winter War experiences was verse. They both left heartbreaking poems about Taipaleen-Joki, but they're written in different keys. That's quite natural as the two poets represent two different sides in the war—the attackers and the defenders. Translation of poetry is a large order and I probably haven't done full justice to either of the poems. But here's how I understood and sensed them. Yrjö Jylhä's poem is beautiful and touching, quite long and I'm offering you the translation of only the final verse. Dolmatovski's, on the contrary, is very short.

Yrjö Jylhä
A Song About A River (the final verse)

Taipaleenjoki, Tuonelanjoki* -
It'll yet turn into a stream of life
When sufferings subside and pain disappears,
Mourning then will as power appear.
Forgetting a lot, understanding much
It'll homeward-bound its sources touch
And lift on its waves the beloved we mourn,
Take them to the heart of the land where born.
Blessing them there, it'll turn back again.
Oh! Who without tears could endure the pain?
So pathetic is the song's round!
But hope and trust know no bounds!
**Tuonelanjoki - River of Death.*

Ye. Dolmatovsky
Recollections of a River

I've seen many a river narrow and wide,
But not every river does memory keep.
There's a Taipaleenjoki, I've been at its side,
A river that's neither wide, nor deep.

But crossing it was a must
That was harder than going through life.
And when the pontoons were up,
Passing the curtain of fire was strife.
But men went on and on quietly, in anger,
And their only thought was, "I'm alive!"
The Volga-natives' thoughts did not on Volga linger:
Only what they saw was life: they had to survive.
A solitary voice was carried by the thunder
Of a wounded in the torrent crying for aid.
And a century-bound wave was carried out yonder
On to the cold and rapid path Taipaleenjoki paved.

THE GREAT PATRIOTIC WAR

Such is the name under which World War II fought on vast Russian and European territories has gone down in history. The Finns in turn have called it "Jatko-sota"—the Continuous War. Small wonder: Only one year, two and a half months separated Hitler Germany's blitzkrieg from the Winter War. That the Soviet Union hadn't drawn the necessary lessons from its actual defeat in the Winter War was evident from the rapid onslaught of the Vermacht.

New losses. New graves. Among them many of Finnish-Americans too.

The "Karelia" publishers have given its readers two editions devoted to losses in the Great Patriotic War. One of them "Eternal Glory to Heroes" saw light in 1992.[17] In the Preface we read:

"Without doubt the lists of those who perished are far from complete. Suffice it to say that in conformity with certain data over 80,000 warriors fell on Karelian territory. At present there are 285 graves in the republic which bear the remains of 35,194 soldiers and officers. The names of 31,798 have been established while only 12,128 have been eternalized on fraternal graves."

This is where fraternal graves can be found today:

Petrozavodsk, Belomorsk, Kalevala (Uhtua), the village of Voinitsa, Kostamus, Vuokkiniemi (all Kalevala, former Uhtua district), Kondopoga, Louhi, Kiestinki, Sovporog, Medvezhyegorsk, Velikaya Guba, Pindushi, the 9th gates of BBK, Maaselkä, Kosmozero, on the road Medvezhyegorsk-

Pudozh, Baryshnavolok, two on the Kochkoma-Rebola road, Rebola, Vidlitsa, on the Pitkäranta-Petrozavodsk road, Ladva-Vetka, near Ramentsy station on the Kirovsk railway; Kuopismaa and Loimola (the Suojärvi district). These are the spots where we could stick in some new flags depicting losses.

Whenever I hear the words "bratskaya mogila" (fraternal grave), they bring to mind the beloved Russian bard Vysotsky's lines from a song bearing the same title:

"Fraternal graves bear no crosses,
Nor do widows come here to weep.
But posterity reveres the losses
With Eternal flames and flowers that keep."

But how many of those who perished were so young that they hadn't even tasted the bitter-sweet emotions of love, so young that they had left behind no widows or children? Still parents, brothers and sisters, devoted friends remained to mourn them, to cherish their memory. American-born men:

Second lieutenant Walter Kataja, b.1919, Ontario, Canada;

Erland Niemi, b.1912, Ironwood, Mich.US;

Raymond Niskanen, b.1917, Vermont, US;

Erkki Männistö, b.1920, Duluth, MN, US;

Walter Heino. b.1916, Menagha, MN, US, buried in the Piskarevskoye Memorial Complex in St.Petersburg;

Karl Reini, 1909, US, buried in Vologda;

John (Juho) Vertti, b.1911, Mass., US. His last resting place is in Rumania;

Karl Sara, b.1910, Palmer, Mich., US;

Eino (Ensio) Suni, b.1920 US, from US 1931;

William Hauskonen (Huuskonen), b.1916, US;

Toivo Mäkelä, b.1911, Worcester, Mass;

Matti Säntti, b.1923, Canada; from Canada 10.12.1931;

Juho Säntti, b.1923, Canada; same arrival date;

The following names belong to men born in Finland, but they came to Karelia from America;

Väinö Paavola, b.1906, arrived from Canada in 1931;

Väinö Saari, b.1891, from Waukegan, Ill. in 1931;

Ensio Panttila; b.1909; from Canada 30.07.33;

Leo Niinisalo, b.1928, Canada, perished when the war was already over: on September, 11, 1945. (The irony of fate: you'll find his father's name in Appendix 3). Leo was working on the clearing of mines. He is the last registered war victim among Finnish-Americans.

The second "Karelia" publication "Book of Memory" saw light in 1994.[18] In this one the burial places are indicated only if they are not on Karelian territory. The Book gives frugal data, inaccurate in some respect, on the person and the place from where he was drafted. Among those who perished there are many who were in partisan detachments and upon being captured by the enemy, they found no mercy. They were sentenced to death and shot immediately. Among them:

Pauli Maunumäki, b.1922, Kirkland Lake, Canada;
Raymond Matson, b.1923, Michigan, USA;
Vilho Suikkanen, b.1924, Port Chester, NY;
Walter Kent, b.1914, New York, US;
Pentti Nuorteva, b.1910, Mass.,USA;
Matti Nuorteva, b.1910, Mass., USA.

Karelian soil has swallowed all the Nuortevas but one—Kerttu, whom you read about in "Red Exodus." Alexander Nuorteva is buried in the Fraternal grave in the center of Petrozavodsk. He had the honestly earned reputation of an international Marxist and was laid to rest with honors in 1928. There's no doubt that, if a serious illness hadn't pulled him down, he'd have shared one of the numerous unknown and unmarked graves of his comrades in the thirties. His sons' remains were buried in a far-off place people seldom visit - Kosmozero.

The "Book of Memory" contains numerous names of Finnish-Americans counted among the missing. They make quite a list. In later research I discovered new names in the Finland military archives, but what actually happened to many others is not clear. War is war! The quicker the onslaught—the more victims! There's a large probability that some men remained lying dead or mortally wounded on the battle field and that they were buried by advancing enemy troops, so their names may yet be discovered in Finland's war-time field hospital papers. But there's another possibility, which can't be excluded,—that of a mortally wounded comrade's papers being extracted by the retreating Russian troops. This is what happened to Superior, Wisconsin-born Akseli Niskanen, 1914. So the search must go on.

Here are names of the known missing:

Einari Kauppi, b.1917, Quincy, Mass.;

John Kauppi, b.1921, Quincy, Mass;
Antti Kylmänen, b.1898, Finland, from Fairport, Ohio;
Erkki Paljakka, b.1915, US;
Erkki Poutu, b.1913, US;
Eino Passonen, b.1903, US;
Leo Kopra, b.US; from US 10.10.1931;
Reino Oinonen; b.1911; from US 1932;
Jorma Bento, b.1913, West Lynn, Mass.;
Toivo Juntunen, b.1923, US;
Kalevi Laine, b.1925, Port Arthur, Canada;
Vilho Lehtinen (Leskinen ?), b.1919, Sault Ste Marie, Canada;
Asser Lekander, 1914, Canada;
Ernest Aalto, 1915, Minn.US;
Matti Tiiainen, 1906, arrived from Kirkland Lake, Canada;
Wäinö Nikkarinen, 1897, from US in 1932;
Pentti Ranta, b.1919, Canada;
Mikko Salo, b.1920, US;
Toivo Piilo, b.1922 (probably Finland); arrived from Fitchburg, Mass., in 1931.
Onni Mikkonen, b.1918, Cape Cod, Mass.;
George Santala, b.1912, US;

Skoklund P., b. Massachusetts; US (this name has not been traced to any other documents but I'm reproducing it exactly the way it stands in "The Book of Memory". In Finland's military archives a SKOGLUND Lenny's death sentence was commuted and he was sent to a POW camp.

Elmer (Ilmari) Kainulainen, b.1922, Canada;
Aarre (Aarne) Putansuu, b.US; from US 1931;
Matti Tiiainen, b.1906, Sortavala (see appendix N 3);
Eino Kivelä; b.1902; from Canada 1932;.
Wilbert Ranta; b.US, 1915; from US 10.11.31;
Ernest Aalto; b.1915, New Hampshire US; from US 1932;
Seppälä Mikko; b.Finland, 1897; from Canada 10.12.31;
Seppälä Erkki Mikko's son; b.1923 Canada;

In the course of reading you've come across the name Kauppi (in some papers they figure as "Kauppinen". The typically Finnish -nen was dropped off many names) from Quincy, Massachusetts, thrice. No mistake! Tiny, soft-spoken Anna Kauppi was left alone after losing all her menfolk. Only

Heikki, the family head, died a natural death: Teddy was a NKVD victim and John and Einari are reported missing.

THE MILITARY ARCHIVES OF FINLAND.

I pinned great hopes on finding valuable information in these archives, as I already knew about young men taken prisoner by the Finnish army. The luckier ones had managed to escape to Sweden and from there to their homelands—the US and Canada. Many such "happy endings" were already known to me and new names were discovered, but I'm not disclosing them. Only the names of those who have passed on are given in the full. Some POWs had been exchanged and returned to the Soviet Union. Like hundreds of thousands of others, they paid for their "crime" with long-term sentences in gulags. Some met with untimely death from the hands of their captors. But each of these cases has to be dealt with separately.

I'd like to begin with an important detail. There undoubtedly existed a status providing for special treatment of POWs, who were not Finland-born. I didn't have the chance to read these papers myself, but from talks with the Archive staff it proved to be so. This explains two things:

First, why death sentences were substituted for life-long imprisonment. This is what happened to my would-be husband Milton Sevander, b.1920, Eveleth, Minn. His death sentence reads: "Heti," which means "to be put into effect immediately." Five hours saved him from the firing squad. Milton Sevander was even included among the names of those executed in Finland in a "Helsingin sanomat" publication. I've read this "Heti" in so many documents, that I've retained an inkling of hope: probably he/she was not executed after all! Second, why, in some cases, Swedish authorities refused to return Soviet prisoners-of-war to Finland for the latter to hand them over to the Soviet military. (On the margin of a paper you can read, "Han är icke Sovjet medborgare"—He is not a Soviet citizen). In one of the papers there is a marking by Finland military authorities to the effect that POW Oiva M. has been released as he is not a Soviet Union citizen.

Two prisoner-of-war cards (sotavankikortti) are reproduced at the end of the chapter: one for Robert Nylander, b.24.06.18, St.Paul, Minnesota. The other for Tauno Ruis, b.22.08.1911, Vancouver, Canada. Robert was transferred to POW camp N 16 in September, 1944, and there's no further information; Tauno died on March 23, 1942, in POW camp N 3.

I knew both of them. The Nylanders lived on the same floor with us in the so-called Hotel in Uritsky Street, Petrozavodsk. Only the youngest two, Doris and Oiva, are among the living today. Heimo was an NKVD victim, Jouko and Robert were lost in the war (there's no information on Jouko!). They even came to arrest the family head Urho Nylander in 1937, but he had died a natural death a few years earlier.

Handsome, broad-shouldered, curly-headed Don, as we knew Tauno Ruis, was dating my pal Ruthy Merila's sister Flossie. How we admired both of them and wished we'd have such imposing boyfriends ourselves some day. Don wasn't only attractive but also a clean-cut worthy man, a good trumpet player in the Symphony and, alas, an only son. Some readers may remember the Meriläs from Grand Rapids, Mich. Florence united her life with another young American man, Tauno Rauhala (Warren, Ohio), who returned after eight years in a gulag. They're doing fine. Flossie will be celebrating her 80th birthday this November.

Now if a researcher could find such cards on one and every prisoner-of-war captured in Finland, the task would be relatively easy. Unfortunately that was not the case. So, if by chance there's a mistake in my judgement about the birthplace of some men executed in Finland in the war years, it's through no fault of mine. I'm relying only on oral data given by relatives and friends.

Thus, the following Americans could have been saved. Saved from what, you may ask. From death caused by a firing squad bullet? Yes! But there's no saying what would have awaited them if they had been exchanged!

Otso-Sakari Laakso, b.1918, Mass., executed 18.01.1942.
Eino-Yrjö Salo, b.1923, Newberry, Mich., executed 30.08.41.
Melvin Laine, b.22.11.16, US, executed (no date).
Esko Rintala, b.1913, Massachusetts, executed 10,09,41.
Britta Niemi, b.1917, Brooklyn, NY, executed 30,09,41.
Reino Wentelä, b.1917, Canada, executed 5.05.42.
William Hevosaho, b.1912, Canada (?) (no date of exec.)
Paavo Saari, b.1914, Waukegan, Ill. (most people remember him by his nickname "Biffo"—an excellent swimmer!), executed 10.09.41.
Aate Pitkänen, b.1913, Port Arthur, Canada; executed 13.06.42.
Viljo Nurminen; b.1921, Canada; from Canada 1932; executed 30.08.41.
Karl Pitkänen; b.1915; from Canada 1931; executed 1.08.41.
Oiva Helin; b.1920 (birthplace indefinite), executed 18.01.42.

The following two men came to Karelia from America, but were born in Finland:

Aate-Einari Urpola, b.4.05.03, from Canada, executed 18.01.42.

Aarre Eskolin, b.23.08.16, Tampere, from Brooklyn, NY, executed 1942.

There's no indication of a sentence passed on

Hannes Utter, b.18.12.19, Duluth Minn. Only a note: "Utter has been handed over to commander of the VI AK 09.01.43."

The same goes for the following men who were sent to other POW camps:

Matias Lehto; b.1893 Finland; from Canada 1931.

Eino Mäenpää; b.1920 Canada; from Canada 1933.

Helge Vainio; b.1922 Canada; from Canada 1932.

Yrjö Wäisänen; b.1904; from Canada 1931.

George Santala; b.1912, US; from US 1932.

Niemi Marvin, b.8.07.22, Iron River, Mich. He was a POW at the Vyborg (Viipuri) POW camp evacuated under heavy fire in 1944. No further information.

Thus I sense a strong probability that the lives of some of these men were saved. That is if "heti" was reversed or if those under consideration survived POW camps. Let's hope so!

World literature abounds in facts when arrests and convictions by counterintelligences often wind up quite unexpectedly. Sometimes it's made public that a person has perished, sometimes a man's fate is falsified or simply silenced. After a stretch of time he may appear in another country, under an assumed identity, working for a foreign intelligence service. American-Finns were not exempt from this adventurous game either. Many of you might have read Kaarlo Tuomi's "Isänmaattoman Tarina" ("The Story of a Man without a Fatherland"). A few Finnish-Americans are in the books of Soviet Intelligence agents, Aileen-Doris Sarkkinen and Reino Häyhänen, to mention but two, besides K.Tuomi. At first I saw no sense in the fact that American birth certificates were confiscated with the arrest of parents. But when I didn't find ours in my father's file, I thought there must have been a purpose. I'm not saying other Mayme, Paul or Aino Corgans appeared somewhere. But who knows? We were not the only ones! Talking with my peers I've learned that the Corgan kids were no exception: confiscating birth certificates appeared to be a common practice.

Here's a little imaginary dialogue between an NKVD officer and prisoner Väinö-Rudolf Ranta, b.1918, Florence, Wisconsin, which, to my mind, wouldn't be a far cry from the truth:

Officer: Do you know what day it is today?

Ranta: Yes.

Officer: You're to be shot. What have you got to say for yourself?

Ranta: I can only repeat: not guilty.

Officer: Well, well, maybe we can do something for you.

Ranta: The sooner you get over with it the better.

Officer: We've given your case serious consideration and have decided to substitute the death sentence for a gulag.

Ranta: I'd prefer dying.

Officer: Who knows, you might change your mind some day.

The long and the short of it is that in NKVD Protocol N 15 we read, "Send Ranta Väinö to Vyatlag (a gulag in the vicinity of the city Vyatka), order N 1277, dated 26.09.38, signed by chief of Petrozavodsk prison Nyuchagin."

My next "contact" with Väinö Ranta was in Finland's Military archives. First he was sentenced to execution 15.12.42, then transferred into the disposal of Commander of Division 17. No further information. The dates leave ample room for speculation. If good luck came his way, he might even be among the living today. I assume such a possibility, as this is what happened to another American K.D., b.1913, New York, who managed to escape from a prison camp in Finland, from there to Sweden and then—Home!

We could replace names in the imaginary dialogue given above:

Eino-Ilmari Matikka, b.in Finland 1901, arrived from Canada in 1933, lived in Santala, Kondopoga district, sentenced to death and executed 02.10.38, in keeping with NKVD Protocol N 11. In Finland his death sentence was also commuted. In Finland's documents Matikka's birth date stands 1908, so there's a slim possibility of two different people having lived in a Karelian lumber camp with the same name!

Matti K., b.Waukegan, Ill., 1907, worked in Kindasovo, Pryazha district, stands in the list of rehabilitated victims (Appendix 1). He, too was captured in Finland, but there's no indication of a sentence. Hopefully, he got away!

Antti Haakana; b.1903, Viipurinl.; from Canada 1932; worked as logger in Segezha district, Losinaya Gora logging camp. Arrested in 1937. Rehabilitated in 92/3. (See app.1) Torkiainen Emil, b.1891, Finland, arrived from Canada in 1931, lived in Kondopoga, death sentence in

NKVD protocol N 3, captured in Finland, returned to the Soviet Union (date not indicated).

A case like that of Emil Torkiainen sets you thinking, that probably Finnish military authorities considered returning him to Russia the harshest sentence that could be passed on a Finland-born captured as a Soviet scout in his native country. Since his arrest in 1938 up to his last breath whenever and wherever he knew nothing but hard sufferings.

The 1944 Paris Peace Treaty between the Soviet Union and Finland provided for the mandatory return of Soviet prisoners-of-war captured in Finland. This was the first step in the following post-war events when, on the basis of similar agreements, hundreds of thousands of prisoners-of-war were returned to Russia from England, France, from the German concentration camps. Ally government heads Roosevelt, Churchill and De Gaulle were severely criticized for this inhuman policy, as Stalin's atrocities were no longer a secret. POWs filled the numerous gaps that had opened in the gulags due to the mass deaths of the purge victims. New gulags were opened!

In "Red Exodus" I gave the names of five such victims: Raymond Leino, Leo Luoma, Toivo Solman, Yrjo Mykkänen and Viola Sandros. The latter two were not returned from Finland, but in connection with German captivity. You can read about them a bit later. I also mentioned the men who had gone through three-four years of filter camps and returned to their families, among them Kalle Kemppainen, Victor Närvä and Milton Sevander. The sad fate of Eino Prykä was also mentioned. I asked for his file in the NKVDA but did not receive it, as it was in the Prosecutor's office for the purpose of rehabilitation. To the names given I'll add:

Men who were in filter camps and returned to their families:

Lauri Hämäläinen, b.1919, Ishpeming, Michigan;

Armas Mustonen, b.1909, Finland, Kemijärvenp., came to Karelia from Canada in 1932(?);

Victor Jokimaki, b.1900, Finland, but arrived from the US in 1931;

Kalle Heinonen, who arrived from Canada. His fate is unknown;

Ensio Haapanen, b.1922, Canada, is known to have visited Petrozavodsk in the post-war years, but he's living somewhere beyond Karelia.

Fred Salonen, b.1925, US, son of the Salonens you've read about.

Harold Hietala; b.1917 Canada and has returned to his native parts.

Viljo Saarinen; b.1917 Nashwauk, Minn. US.

Nothing is known of the fates of the following American-born who were exchanged:

Toivo Ovaskainen, b. 8.10.16, US;

Frank Pajunen, b.13.12.12, Yorkville, Ohio;

John Björklund; b.1923, US; from US 1932.

There's one person in this list of returned POWs I'd like to say a few words about. He's not Finnish, he's not American, but his whole life was connected with Finns, with whom he had formed strong bonds.

Jan Repak, b.11.12.1898, Austria. For some reason or other he got hooked on the Finnish language, took a great liking to Finns whom life had brought him into contact with, and moved to Finland in his early youth. But his choice of time wasn't a good one: the Civil War in Finland with the persecution of friends who were making plans to escape to Canada. He threw his lot in with theirs and thus found himself in Canada. And then, once again, when the call for Karelia resounded he joined his comrades and came to Karelia in 1932. People who knew him claim his Finnish was irreproachable. But what amazes me in this person's life is that I found him in the list of returnees from Karelia to Canada. Adventurer that he was, he might have returned to Finland in the Winter War. It's known that huge numbers of volunteers signed up from many countries to go to little Finland's help. The last known of him is that in 1944 he was turned over to Soviet military authorities in the exchange process. Amazing, isn't it?

Strange and unknown is the final fate of

Sulo Autio, b.1920, Marquette, Mich.;

Eino Siikki, b.1910, Wisc., US;

Arvo Vaara, b.28.01.91, Finland, Vaasanl., Teuva; arrived to Karelia from Canada.

In 1941 these three POWs were handed over to the Germans. I couldn't get an answer to the question, why this had happened. The only further information on any of them is that Sulo Autio fell seriously ill with pneumonia and was hospitalized in Tallinn by the Germans. Then what? Miracles do sometimes occur. Could it be that these men found their way to freedom through Germany?

Readers may have answers to the numerous questions I'm posing. I'd appreciate hearing from such people. I pledge confidentiality.

Have I managed to bring home to the reader why I call beautiful Karelia a graveland?

There are only two definite figures: 800,000 victims in the construction of the White Sea Canal. We do not have the number of victims of the Solovki and other Belomorsk gulags. Over 80,000 perished in WWII. The tragedies of the Winter War still remain to be objectively counted. You don't have to stretch your imagination to get thousands of other victims to realize that Karelia is soaked in the blood of innocent people.

That was not the land our parents were taking us to. They hoped to help in creating a land of free labor and plenty, they counted on giving their offspring a good education, they looked forward to a happy life.

But that was not to be!

The graves of My People scattered all over Karelia number in hundreds. No one knows how many were left in distant places all over Russia in the years of evacuation.

Remaining members of immigrant families don't even see each other very often nowadays. But you're sure to meet when one of our peers or nonagenarians is seen to his last resting place. Not even a year has passed since friends and family bid farewell to nonagenarians Aarne Rikka and Wilho Hakala. This is happening more and more seldom... The older generation has passed away, our peers are returning to their homelands or to Suomi from where our parents once took off for the enticing lands of America. In many families the third generation is following their American-born parents. Not many of My People remain in Karelia.

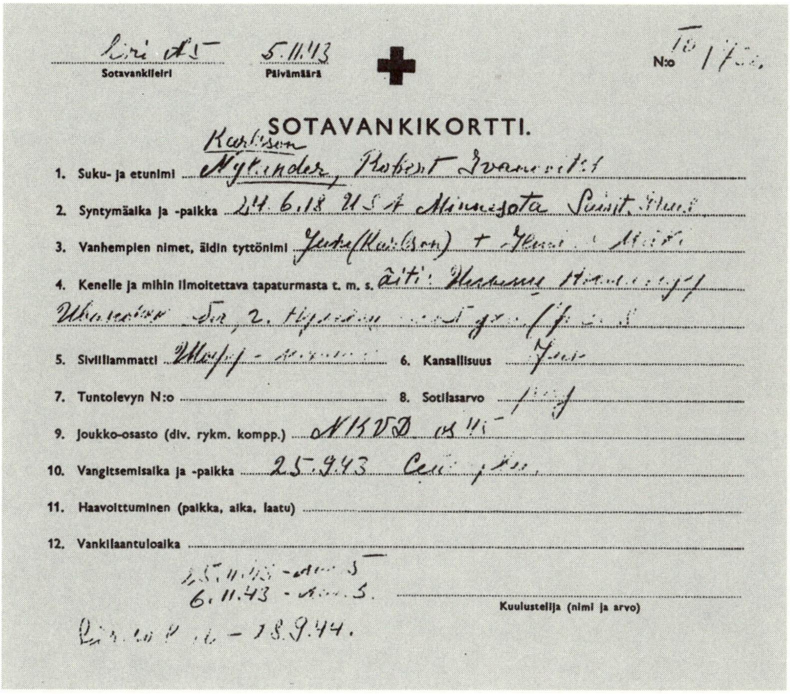

Leiri № 5 — Sotavankileiri
5.11.43 — Päivämäärä
N:o [illegible]

SOTAVANKIKORTTI.

1. Suku- ja etunimi Nylander (Karlsson), Robert Ivanovitš
2. Syntymäaika ja -paikka 24.6.18 U.S.A. Minnesota [illegible]
3. Vanhempien nimet, äidin tyttönimi Juho (Karlsson) + [illegible]
4. Kenelle ja mihin ilmoitettava tapaturmasta t. m. s. äiti: [illegible]
[illegible]
5. Siviiliammatti [illegible]
6. Kansallisuus [illegible]
7. Tuntolevyn N:o
8. Sotilasarvo [illegible]
9. Joukko-osasto (div. rykm. kompp.) NKVD [illegible]
10. Vangitsemisaika ja -paikka 25.9.43 [illegible]
11. Haavoittuminen (paikka, aika, laatu)
12. Vankilaantuloaika

[illegible] — 6.11.43 — [illegible]
[illegible] — 18.9.44.

Kuulustelija (nimi ja arvo)

Sv. — Sv. järj. tai sv. leiri N:o
20.10.41. — Päivämäärä
Kotij. E.*)
Vangin N:o 1/7.850 5C II b.

SOTAVANKIKORTTI.

1. Suku- ja etunimi Ruis, Tauno Alfredinpoika,
2. Syntymäaika ja -paikka 22.8.1911, Kanada-Vancouver,
3. Vanhempien nimet, äidin tyttönimi Alfred, Vilhelmiina Vilander,
4. Kenelle ja mihin ilmoitettava tapaturmasta t. m. s. Äiti: Vilhelmiina Ruis, Petroskoi Solomennoje, Skalistaja katu 17,
5. Siviiliammatti Trumpetin soittaja
6. Kansallisuus Amerikan Suomal.
7. Tuntolevyn N:o
8. Sotilasarvo Punaarmeijalainen.
9. Joukko-osasto (div. rykm. kompp.) Erill. tiedust. osasto № 4093.
10. Vangitsemisaika ja -paikka 3.10.41 Hyrsylä.
11. Vankilaantuloaika 9.10.41.
12. Vanki lähetetty edelleen (milloin ja minne) Joap. sv. leiri 14:sta 30.11.41.

*) Tämä kortti lähetetään aina vangin mukana sijoituspaikkaan.

(Käännä)

8 True Stories.

THE FORCE OF FAITH

A letter from Switzerland! I'd have been totally perplexed but for knowing of the strangest way Viola Sandros (the next story) had learned about "Red Exodus" from Robert Taylor, an Englishman living in Switzerland.

While working on "Red Exodus" now and then I heard remarks like, "Your writings won't interest anyone but you Finns." Time has proved this opinion to be erroneous. I've received a number of appreciative letters from non-Finns who think otherwise. Robert Taylor and his wife Audrey stand out among them. They are people of faith who regard this life as a temporary one preparing Man for Eternity. They do what they can to alleviate the sufferings unjustly heaped upon people and attach the greatest importance to the efforts of one and all to overcome evil and make justice triumph.

In their letter the Taylors write: "Your research and writings are absolutely necessary, for they are a vital testimony of a terrible period in the history of mankind. They are a testimony of great suffering and sacrifice, but also of great courage, love and loyalty. We don't think that any sacrifice, no matter how little or how great, is in vain. In some way it ennobles and enhances the human dignity of the ones who are sacrificed and will ultimately humble those who sought to humiliate their fellow beings."

Needless to say how encouraging such evaluations are, especially when at moments I felt bogged down with the weight of the tragic truth I was unearthing. I do admit there were times when the thought occurred to me that probably my endeavors were useless: why not just wind up with "Red Exodus"? But letters of support, like those of the Taylors, gave me wings. I had to go on!

What a small place the world is. Years ago Robert Taylor met Finnish students for the first time as a teacher in a Swiss school. This first contact served as an impact for his deep interest in the history and culture of Finland, of this little country that produced such industrious young people as his students. Once, just by chance, he heard a short interview with a Stalinist victim on the BBC. The essence of the tragic story of a complete stranger produced a deep impression on him and aroused a sincere desire to help.

It was Robert Taylor who brought me the story of Heimo Rautiainen and family. Knowing the Rautiainens had arrived in Russia on the Gripsholm that sailed out of New York harbor on September 1, 1932, they were also included in my search list. From other Finnish-Americans whose personal tragedies had taken them to Karaganda, Kazakhstan,—Walter Warwick, Suoma Laine, Hank Kari—I learned about another family that evil fate had settled there—the Rautiainens. Heimo was a retired taxi-driver. I made several attempts to establish ties with him, but in vain: no response. No sad feelings on my part. It wasn't the first time I came up against a brick wall of silence or even point-blank refusals of the type, "I don't want to talk about the past," or "I don't appreciate what you are doing." Besides I now know that Heimo's story was coming out, as you'll see.

Heimo and his wife Lyia in their home.

There's no way to measure pain and sufferings. Some people can take more, others—less. I'll never stop wondering how men, who spent the best years of their lives in Stalinist incarceration, and are among us today keep on smiling. But still there must be a limit to how much a person can endure! Heimo's cup of bitterness was overbrimming: the arrest and loss of Father, the arrest of Mother, army conscription with fascist Germany's attack on the Soviet Union, then rejection from active service in the army followed by isolation and the hardships of one of

Heimo and his mother Maria-Sigrid celebrating Easter, shortly before she passed away in their Karaganda home.

the numerous labor camps (LC) in Central Asia, the death of his eldest son, looking after an old and ailing mother, who had survived the gulag. Due to the tender care of loving son and family, Maria Sigrid Rautiainen lived to be a nonagenarian.

The pattern, if not the number, of Heimo's tragedies resembles that of many others. It was not for nothing that in "They Took My Father" I reproduced Oscar Corgan's two death certificates: every family that applied for a death certificate a second time received an identical one with place of death not indicated, cause of death—shot. It was not for nothing that in "Red Exodus" I gave a lengthy description of LC's, to which representatives of national minorities were sent to toil and... die. It was not for nothing that in a few families, as well as in that of Heimo Rautiainen, parents recommended their children to give up their Finnish identity to save themselves from possible persecution in future.

Iron River, Michigan, cirka 1930, from left Heimo, Father-Emil and mother-Maria.

Who knows, life might have treated Heimo and family with more mercy if they could have left Kazakhstan behind and moved to another place. But even that was out of the question: former political prisoners were not allowed to change places of residence. You had to wait ten years!

Heimo was born on May 8, 1921 in Thunder Bay, Canada,

but the family arrived in Russia from Iron River, Michigan. Emil Rautiainen had become a US citizen as early as in 1916. Upon receiving US citizenship he served in the American Marines. For a brief period of time the family lived in Canada but returned shortly to Michigan, where they remained up to the moment of their departure to Soviet Russia. Emil was a qualified specialist in ventilation and sheet metal working. There was no doubt that such a man would have no trouble finding a job. Emil was appreciated, but that didn't stop the NKVD from arresting him. High qualification sometimes even served as a cause for the arrest: NKVD were in need of highly qualified labor and not only men to fell trees and dig ditches. Though that was not Emil Rautiainen's fate: his life was cut short by an executioner's bullet.

Robert wrote to Heimo. His first question was whether there was any way in which he could help Heimo's family. The answer was short, "Help us get out. We are ready to go anywhere beyond the boundaries of Russia." A tall order, taking into consideration that Heimo had no identity papers whatsoever. He couldn't prove his parents' citizenship nor marriage status, the circumstances of his own birth. He had already turned to the Canadian Embassy in Moscow but on learning about the papers he was to submit he just gave up the whole idea as unrealistic.

Heimo was in a stage of mental prostration at the time the Taylors contacted him. Thus the large order was shifted to Robert's shoulders. Meanwhile Stephen Handelman, a Moscow bureau "Toronto Star" correspondent had interviewed Heimo in his Karaganda home and published a revealing article in "The Spectator" of April 20, 1991: "A Terrible Mistake." Hopefully it would catch the eye of a knowing person and he would respond. That didn't happen but it brought the sad story of several Finnish-Americans living in Karaganda to the attention of Canadian readers and opened another window in the endless series of Stalinist crimes. How many of them yet remain to be opened!

Even the shortest enumeration of all Robert's undertakings would take a lot of space. I'll limit myself to a brief description to prove how he spared neither time nor efforts to give his new-found friend a helping hand. Now the friends he had made in Finland also came to his assistance in trying to finding Heimo's relatives in Finland but without success. Guided by old addresses, still saved in Heimo's family, Robert located living relatives in the US, Heimo's birth certificate and his parents' marriage certificate. Heimo was amazed to learn that the very house where they had lived in Thunder

Bay, 345 Wilen Street, still stood intact. It bore his grandfather's name: Peter Oxman's Poolroom.

Before 1992 expired, thanks to Robert Taylor and the numerous people whom he had got involved in Finland, Canada and the US, Heimo already had all the required documents, which proved his Canadian citizenship.

All this time the Taylors maintained a lively correspondence with Heimo and family. They were extremely considerate and generous sending packages and money all along to keep the family afloat in trying times when pensions in the former Soviet Union don't suffice to keep body and soul together.

Robert Taylor's exchange of correspondence and contact with the Moscow and Bern Canadian Embassies was also extremely lively. He was taken seriously by the Embassy staffs and regarded as Heimo Rautiainen's one and only counselor and advocate. He was also the one to undertake all the expenses involved. Now they had reached the stage when it only remained for Heimo to go to the Canadian Embassy to receive his passport and leave the country.

Robert Taylor launched his research in April 1991 when he turned to the BBC to obtain Heimo's address. One of the last letters written by the Taylors to Lydia, Heimo's wife, is dated January 27, 1994. It is a letter of condolence. Heimo had breathed his last on September 30, 1993. In this letter the Taylors wrote, "Heimo had a lovely dream in those last two years and a few people were trying to make that dream come true. We have a loving Father in Heaven who used me as His instrument to help to awaken this dream... Heimo is now back in his real Home. I know that this is the truth. That Home is much more beautiful than anything he could've seen here in Switzerland or Finland or Canada or anywhere here on Earth.There are so many beautiful places and lovely people in all countries, but Heimo will suffer no more. He is once more with his mother and father, with his son, his grandparents and his friends, oh, so many people for whom he has cared and who have cared for him."

Reading the quoted excerpt made me feel small. The offspring of radical Finnish-American idealists were taught to believe in a paradise on Earth, to work towards it. We were not church-goers. God and Heaven were Utopias. We don't possess the Taylors' strong convictions, their faith in the Hereafter. The ideals that were instilled in us since childhood suffered many a strong blow, they were gradually crushed. And they have left a void that is not easy to fill. We cannot behave like the Russian Communist party functionaries who were instrumental in destroying churches and the clergy and have now all of a sudden become staunch Orthodox believers, supporters of religion. When were they lying? Then or now?

Thank you, Robert and Audrey. You, your convictions and efforts, your protegees are certainly honored on earth too. Hopefully many will follow suit and "do unto others as you'd have them do unto you!"

A FINNISH-AMERICAN GERMAN

Sulo, Aili and Viola Sandros; Detroit, 1922

A young girl, student of the Leningrad Institute of Foreign Languages, was summoned to the dean's office. Besides the dean himself, there were two strangers: a good-looking young man and an unpleasant character in his fifties. Both men eyed her with apparent interest. They liked what they saw: a pretty blue-eyed blond who held herself upright with a sense of dignity. The elder stranger got on his feet, offered his hand and muttered something in the line of a self-introduction. The dean invited everyone to be seated and excused himself saying duty called him elsewhere, so he'd leave them not to be in the way during their little chat.

No sooner had he departed than the stranger's stern face broke into smiles and, rubbing his hands, he declared:

"Just what we need—Aryans, the choice couldn't be a better one. So here's what it's all about." Then followed introductions. The young man appeared to be a Sudet German studying at the Leningrad Physical Training Institute (Lesgaft). Even though it wasn't love at first sight both young people took a liking to each other and a sense of mutual confidence was born then and there. Naturally decision-making became easier and safer.

This was 1940. Both had a perfect command of their native tongues: Viola—English and Finnish, Emil—German, to say nothing of Russian which was the language of instruction. Viola was majoring in English.

The autumn of 1940! The date speaks for itself: unrest in the world since the advent of Hitler and his brown shirts to power. Poland and Czechoslovakia were already occupied by the Nazis and black clouds kept hovering over Europe. Strange things were happening in the Soviet Union: its take-over of former Polish territories under the guise of "reunification;" the incomprehensible Winter War; the reinforcement of Soviet troops along the new USSR borders in the three Baltic States. There was much ado about "a threat from the West," but very little talk about "Drang nach Osten," which, as we know, led to the Pact of Non-Aggression between the Soviet Union and Germany in 1940. This Pact was to have given the Soviets time to prepare for any possible onslaught. But reality proved otherwise.

Talking about young people who agreed to become Soviet reconnaissance agents, the political situation cannot be overlooked. The threat of Nazism which was wiping out whole territories, exterminating non-Aryan population, foremostly Jews and Poles, was obvious. Thus resistance to the black forces of reaction to save the world was a motif recruiters could take advantage of. Scouting in the German rear was more than dangerous, but it acquired a comprehensible romantic aspect that brought forward honest and daring adventure-loving people in all countries, threatened by Hitlerism. Probably the heroic struggle of the French Resistance is the most widely-known example one could quote; so much has been written about it!

Viola and Emil were no exception. They also considered it their duty to take part in the battle to save the world and after some consideration agreed to play the role mapped out for them: Emil—that of a scout in his home parts—Sudetenland, where the population was German, Viola—that of his radio-operator.

Viola spent several months at a scout school somewhere not far from Moscow. There she received papers identifying her as a Finnish citizen. In December 1940 she met Emil Kammler in Tallinn and that's where their marriage was registered. Marriage to a German entitled her to German citizenship too. She got her German passport and in December the young couple boarded a boat and sailed to his home country.

They understood what they were in for: on Sudet territory they were to supply Soviet intelligence with information on the deployment and transportation of German troops.

When Emil and Viola Kammler settled down in Kratzau, Czechoslovakia, she was an expectant mother. Their son was born on January 7, 1942. Unfortunately, Emil had no chance to participate in the upbringing of his son: he was drafted and dispatched to the Eastern front where he perished without having served the interests of the Soviet Intelligence.

Viola was left alone with her little Siegfried, but it was a good thing that Emil's relatives were around to give her material and moral support. They endured the difficulties that became the lot of the local population under the fascists but luckily Viola's true identity was never discovered and she survived.

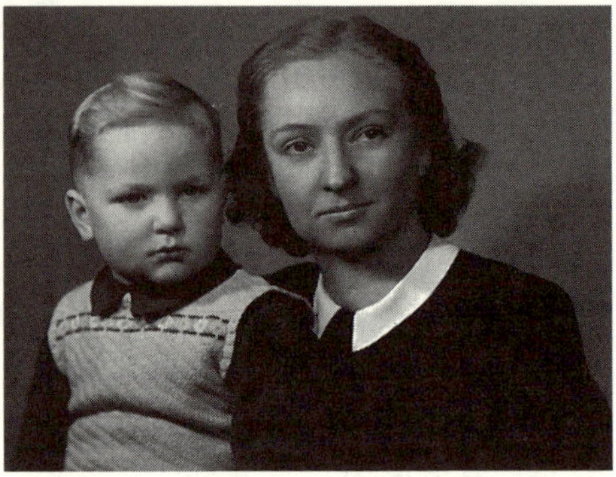

Viola and Siegfried just before Viola went to the Soviet embassy in Prague, 1945

When Victory Day came, her first thoughts were to find family: her parents—father Sulo and mother Aili, aunt Hilja's family, all of whom she had left in Karelia, without knowing anything of their wartime life. She was to learn about that many years later, only after she drew another circle of dreadful experiences, only after her folks had given her up as lost for ever!

The only wise step to take, she thought, was to turn to the help of the Soviet Embassy in Prague. She was after all a Soviet citizen, whom duty had called to parts of the world she would have normally never have found herself in. Viola had a clean conscience: she hadn't done anything to smear her citizenship obligations. The new unexpected circumstances of her life were not of her own making.

One beautiful early summer day in 1945 she left her three-and-a-half-year-old son in the care of Emil's relatives and set off for the Embassy. What a good thing she didn't take him along! I'm sure it would have been the last she'd have ever seen of him. He, like many other "orphans," would have found himself either in a new family or in an orphan home.

The reception was without incident. Viola only had to repeat her story, as an officer of higher rank was invited the second time and it was he who took her away. Quite unexpectedly she soon found herself in a Soviet camp in Baden, not far from Vienna. With other women she shared a room without furniture, only hay-stuffed mattresses on the floor and a toilet in the corner. Two months passed peacefully at this "summer residence," from where she and the other inmates were transferred to Lemberg (Poland), a former Jewish ghetto, taken over by the Russians. When a sentence was read out to a prisoner, he/she was dispatched to a camp in Russia. In Lemberg Viola was working at a hospital. A year passed before her turn came. She learned that a troika in Moscow had passed a five-year sentence on her for "betraying" her "native land." The two-month long trip began in August, 1946. It ended in Norilsk, which alongside with Magadan, Dudinka, Komi, Kazahkstan and other parts of the country, have gone down in the history of the Soviet Union as places of mass imprisonment and deaths. Only, as usual, she didn't get away with five years. They were followed by another four, which, who knows, might have dragged out even longer but for the belated death of the "great" Stalin!

In Dudinka, where she landed for mandatory settlement after the five-year prison term, she met another sufferer like herself and they decided survival would be easier together. So two became one and a lovely girl was born to them in this cold, desolate, God-forsaken place. They both realized the day for separation would come if his family had survived and was waiting for him. It happened, but Viola had a great consolation—lovely Sylvia. Only recently has this grown-up young lady got to know that her father is alive and living in Estonia. They've established contact and Sylvia's on the verge of departing there for a vacation to make the acquaintance of her father and siblings.

The first exchange of letters Karelia-Dudinka was a mixture of joy and grief. Viola was alive! She had family both in Germany and there, way up north. But Viola was to learn that her father had died of hunger in a labor camp. Sulo Sandros had known four years of unemployment in Detroit and under pressure of his wife Aili (Viola's biological mother had passed away in her infancy but she was blessed with a good step-mother) he finally agreed and signed up for emigration to Karelia. Bitter were the tears of resentment Viola shed thinking of all the tragedies her family had had to endure! But she had to go on living: she was now the only one responsible for Mother, Sylvia and Siegfried, about whose whereabouts she knew nothing.

Upon release Viola travelled to Karelia where Mother, Aunt Hilja and her beloved cousin Sylvia Makinen, with whom she shared happy childhood memories from Detroit, Michigan, were waiting. It was a tearful but happy reunion. Viola's search for her son began without delay. And she found him in the foster family of the same distant relatives. They also had a story to tell.

There might have been a leak of information concerning Siegfried's parents through some channel, because, as soon as peace came and with it the creation of the USSR-maintained and guarded German Democratic Republic, Siegfried and his foster parents were deported to the new part of Germany. That's where Viola found them and upon receiving an invitation to arrive with her daughter, she lost no time getting there. Today Siegfried Kammler is a highly respected urologist with a practice of his own in Bernburg, Germany. I wasn't surprised to learn that he had an adopted son. I believe the loss of both parents had inspired him to help another boy who had found himself in a similar position. Regardless of all her sufferings, the thing Viola regrets most of all is the irretrievable loss of 12 years of companionship with her adored son. To prevent such a thing from happening again, Viola with her newly founded family settled down in Germany for good. Some years later she met a wonderful man and they married. But for his serious illness I could say they are sharing a happy life. Daughter and son with families are frequent visitors, and every minute of their company is cherished.

Viola's story would be incomplete if I didn't let the reader know what a strong, determined person she is. Schooling being left unfinished she took it up again and at the age of 50 graduated from the Friedrich Schiller University in Jena with flying colors working her way through school. (She taught English and Russian at German schools). Now she's enjoying a good government pension, the calm and beauty of her third adopted land, the proximity of family. Mother Aili returned to America, to Thunder Bay, to be exact, where her sister lived. That is where Viola saw her last during her 1973 visit to Canada.

I'm only five years younger than Viola. Today this age difference is non-existent, but in the thirties—what a gap! My peers and I were worthless nincompoops, as compared to Viola and her circle but they never put on airs and we respected them for it. We didn't belong to this set of gorgeous Americans who were admired for many things, singing, dancing and swimming among them. How well I remember Viola, her cousin Sylvia, or Sliver, as she was known, Britta Niemi, Alice Välimaa-Ketola and their beautiful crawl strokes which taught us a lesson or two!

Sliver soldiered through World War II and passed away in 1983 in Tallinn. Pretty, smiling Britta was executed by a Finnish firing squad as a prisoner-of-war. Somehow it seems to me that she kept on smiling to the last.

I finally had the good luck (thanks to Detroitean Kaisa Siimes who in her nineties has returned to her native Tampere) to bring Detroit-born Viola and Alice together after a separation of nigh 60 years. Now they're in touch. Alice, whom I met in her cozy Helsinki home, is just as pretty as ever. She's lost some of her beautiful hair, but she's still singing! Life's great if you don't weaken.

Viola's son Dr. Siegfried Kammler, a specialist in urology. Germany, 1994.

Viola with daughter Sylvia and grandson Miron. Germany, 1995.

Sulo Sandros in the title role of "Kullervo" on the Detroit Hall stage, circa 1930.

The reader might recall that in "Red Exodus" I mention having heard Viola was doing well. This news came from a mutual friend without details. But the lively exchange of letters we are maintaining today became possible only thanks to Robert Taylor, about whom you've read. He made the acquaintance of Viola and husband during their visit to Switzerland. Later, while in the US, he obtained "Red Exodus." Viola knew nothing about it. Discovering Viola's name on p.153, he called her asking whether she knew a Mayme Sevander. "No," she said, "but there was a Mayme Corgan in Petrozavodsk." The rest is easy to figure out and you've already read about what a great man Robert Taylor is. It's truly a small world, isn't it?

Viola and family are now catching up on their Finnish identity. It wasn't easy to locate their relatives in Finland but Aunt Hilja was of great help and they've managed. After the first visit in 1961 with Siegfried, they made a point of travelling there every two–three years. Sylvia has become a frequenter too. They are discovering the beauty and the rich culture of Suomi, improving on the language — everything has become an extremely rich experience for which they are thankful. It's with a deep sense of pride that daughter, like Mother, claims Finnish identity. They realize how much they have to be proud of.

How I'm looking forward to seeing this happily reunited family some day!

BLUE-EYED IDEALIST

The family name Mykkänen stems from the Finnish word "mykkä" meaning "mute, dumb." Paavo Voutilainen's article in a "Carelia" issue begins with the words, "Yrjö Mykkäsen on ollut pakko mykistyä"— "Yrjö Mykkänen was forced to turn dumb."

Paavo Voutilainen, a talented Karelian journalist, drew the portrait of the youngest member of the David and Agatha Mykkänen family, that set forth for the Soviet Union on board the Drottingholm from Halifax on June 22, 1931. Yrjö is one of the many who has taken hard knocks but hasn't succumbed and keeps his sunny side up. To my mind, Paavo's poem, my translation of which he has graciously permitted to publish, tells Yrjö's lifelong story in a unique fashion. There's another detail from Paavo's article that I'd like to add. It concerns Yrjö's character. While serving his term in a Russian gulag Yrjö had saved the life of a POW from Finland—Matti Hirvonen from Joensuu. Matti made Yrjö promise that if he ever set foot in Finland, he was to look him up. So on Yrjö's first visit to the neighboring country, a Finnish journalist, who displayed natural interest in Yrjö's tricky fate, tried to place a call to Matti Hirvonen. There turned out to be five men bearing the same name. One was quick to ask, "Tell me what your left hand looks like." Yrjö's response, "Fingers missing," left no doubt. The happy reunion of these two war-time pals was shown on Finland TV.

Paavo Voutilainen

You're a Blue-Eyed Idealist
Just what
the son of a Finland "punikki"
should be!
You've always believed
in a bright future
and you've always enjoyed
your motley life:
in infancy — in Finland
liberated by the Whites
as a kid —
in depression-stricken Canada;
As a teenager—
in Karjala
where hatred towards Finns was rife;
as a youth—
a German prisoner of war in Viena
and in Siberia—
as a "traitor of the Soviet land";
as a mature man—
in rushing to Communism Soviet Karijala;
spending the summer
fishing worthless fish
teeming in Maasjärvi
spending the winter
in a peeking into Capitalism Petroskoi.

Your work and hobbies
have left no time
to complain of our unlucky fate;
and you haven't become
a returnee
to be fed by others.
You've been to visit
your native Finland now and then,
but you have remained the family's last
blue-eyed idealist
in this land
that's taken more from you
than it has given.
But you don't give a rap
and go on believing in a bright future
and wear an impish smile,
twirling your moustache,
thinking of the chores of the morrow.

You've collected and carved
numberless
new wooden spoons;
maybe just in case
immature Communism should win in Russia.

But what more
could a blue-eyed
idealist wish for?

THE UNITED STATES — RUSSIA — SWEDEN

Sometimes help in finding a person you've been looking for comes from the most unexpected quarter. Reading the December 26, 1993 issue of the local Petrozavodsk "Severny Kuryer" my eye caught the name

Thelma Skinkis. The Christian name set a bell ringing while "Skinkis" meant nothing whatsoever. "Thelma" was imprinted in my memory as belonging to a Detroit-born girl who had come to Russia with her parents at the age of two. I wasn't even sure what her family name was as her parents had divorced and people who had known her claimed there was no further news of the family. The essence of the newspaper article was the following.

The life of a three-year old Karelian girl, Nastya Ylinen by name, had been saved due to heart surgery in Stockholm. She had been invited for treatment with all expenses paid including a two-month stay of both parents. It's always a treat to discover that there are caring people in the world, especially when a child's life is at stake. "Who are those giving people," thought I, "who went to no end of trouble and expenses to perform such a wonderful deed"? "Druzya poznayutsa v bede"—Troubles are the test of friendship! And such was the case, The editorial office gave me the address of the Ylinen family and I lost no time in going to see them to make sure the Stockholm lady was "my" Thelma. By this time I had already established her family name, so I had something to go by. My two books and explanations made it easy to convince the Ylinens of the sincerity of my mission to find Thelma Ojala. It turned out that little Nastya's granny had spent many awful years in a Stalinist gulag. Those who survived never lost touch with each other. In some way or other good fortune had taken one of them to Sweden, so when disaster came knocking at the Ylinen's door, Nastya's granny sent Thelma an SOS explaining the situation and asking for help.

In Stockholm Thelma has a good friend Sinikka, who also took the child's helpless state close to heart. The two of them lost no time. They went from door to door explaining the plight of the child and the urgency of the case. Even they themselves were greatly surprised to discover the readiness of friends and absolute strangers to do their bit. In a short time they collected the fabulous sum of 155,000 Swedish crowns. On getting the little girl's medical case from Petrozavodsk they visited the hospital, talked with the surgery department doctors and got the go-ahead: everything was set for reception and surgery.

The immediate surgery was a success and Nastya became the pet of the department. Her ward was filled with flowers, toys, "Get-well" cards; the local papers thanked their readers for their kindness and wished them well. Nastya will soon turn six. She's doing fine. She has many beautiful things and pictures to remind her of the wonderful "dyady" and "tyoty (uncles and aunts) she has in another country. Such is the story of little Nastya.

Now I had to find Thelma to learn of her adventures, her family. She is one of us. Soon the Swedish mail carried "Red Exodus" to Thelma with my letter enclosed. I asked her to read p.111 with Lempi Tolonen's and my "passportization" experiences, promising, with her permission, to describe her vicissitudes, which make ours, at least mine, seem insignificant.

Thelma's story. Werner Viitaniemi was a highly qualified General Motors worker in Detroit. Like thousands of others, the Great Depression deprived him of his job, so he began looking for new opportunities. That was 1931 when recruitment for Karelia was at its highest point. He had plenty of working class experience and adhered to the lofty ideals expounded by communism. "Why not," he thought, "make the trip to Russia like many others and work there? With my abilities there'll surely be things to do. So why not help that first-born country of working people get on its feet"? His wife Elli wasn't mad about the idea but she had nothing against it either after a hand-to-mouth existence, as the family lived on unemployment benefits. The only ones to put their foot town was family: Elli's aunt and uncle—Ida and John Laine and Werner's half-sister Olga Raymond. They were indignant at the idea of taking little Thelma to Russia. They actually begged to leave the child to them, to go to see for themselves, and, only if everything looked safe, to come back to fetch the child. But no mother will voluntarily be separated from her child especially when there doesn't seem to be any cause for concern.

On May 15, 1931 among numerous other passengers to Karelia the Kungsholm carried the Viitaniemis from the port of New York on this unpredictable voyage. Things went wrong from the start. The Viitaniemis were not only up against the usual odds that every family had to endure. There was friction among the adults which soon led to separation. Elli shortly remarried. Her second husband was Matti Ojala from Finland, an able man and, as Thelma recalls, a very kind and considerate stepfather. She considers herself fortunate to have had two good fathers, who thought the world of her and were both kind and loving. Both men, by the way, knew each other, as they were employed at the same plant in Petrozavodsk.

In 1938 the Ojalas lived in Matrosa. Thelma recalls how on a beautiful summer day Werner came to see them. Sitting on Daddy's knees Thelma listened to his regrets and apologies for having brought them to Russia and his strong advice to try and get back, or at least see Thelma return to her homeland safe and sound. For already a year innocent people had been disappearing day by day. Werner claimed that many Onega tractor plant workers were among them and that he had the feeling his turn would come soon.

Only a week passed and this premonition turned into devilish reality. Werner was nabbed at the factory gates and driven home in a Black Maria, where a so-called search was made. The only "incriminating facts" that were established and taken away were the first class tools he had brought along from the States. Never again was anything heard of Werner. Only recently has it been established that he was sentenced by one of the numerous troikas, and executed.

Misfortunes come in flocks. A week later Matti Ojala received a subpoena from the NKVD. (A very refined way of conducting arrests. This happened to several victims.) He was to show up there on a definite day and hour. Elli got some things together, just in case, she said, and went to see him off to the "Grey House" to which city folk had already got accustomed to giving a wide berth. Try as he would to calm her, to ensure her that nothing would happen, that they'd let him go as they'd soon discover that they were dealing with an innocent man, anxiety prevailed. Matti Ojala wasn't an exception: every detainee considered himself invulnerable and innocent. The words of Stalin, "the great navigator," as he was called by the grovelling media, "Innocent people are not arrested in the Soviet Union," were reiterated time and again. But by this time the purges had already swept away thousands (millions, in reality, but nobody knew!) and such a manner of thinking was already outdated. How strange human nature is: the shoe doesn't pinch until it's on your own foot!

The loss of Werner, her child's father, and Matti, her husband, would have been quite enough for one little family, but nothing doing! The worst was still ahead of Elli: the loss of her only daughter.

At the time the two men were arrested, Thelma had not yet turned nine. The hardships of war and the post-war period were still in store. Werner's words kept ringing in Thelma's ears and, when she received a letter from her aunt in Detroit, she decided it was time to act. Her aunt wrote that Thelma need worry about nothing. She only had to turn to the US Embassy and apply for US citizenship, get a passport and return to her homeland, where she'd be taken good care of. Instead of taking a passport at the mandatory age of 16 (in Russia), Thelma left for Moscow where she was warmly received at the US Embassy and given a paper with the big red seal of the State Department certifying her American citizenship. On returning to Sortavala, where they lived at the time, she turned to the local militia department where she was granted a temporary residential permit. Thelma couldn't stand the idea of leaving Mother alone. But up to this day she can't explain what she was actually counting on, just hoping against hope that the important paper with the imposing red seal spelled protection. So Thelma kept on refusing to take Soviet citizenship and started working. But things changed, she felt that she was under surveillance, especially after the visit of a Finnish-American lady from Petrozavodsk, who expressed curiosity in everything that concerned Thelma and her future plans.(A few names of such people have emerged during my research but for clearly comprehensible reasons I can't mention them). Besides, here's what Thelma herself has to say on the subject, "I don't blame her. To save their own life and those of family some people became informers. But they too are victims. I know nothing about that lady, but if she's still living, I wish her happiness." Is everyone capable of such Christian all-forgiveness? Can it be acknowledged and appreciated? If the answer is positive, it's my opinion that only those who have experienced great sufferings themselves are actually capable of such a noble act.

After this lady's memorable visit there no longer was an attempt to keep the surveillance in secret: one and the same man was constantly in Thelma's field of observation. But the decisive step was taken in the summer of 1948. Thelma was in Petrozavodsk taking cinema mechanic courses. Shortly before they ended she turned to the director with a request to have her residential permit prolonged as it was running out. Upon his advice she turned to the city militia authorities with the same request. They were pretty nice about it there and told her not to worry, that as she was permanent resident of Sortavala, she just had to go to the militia upon arrival and no problem! They'd prolong her residential permit then and there. But Thelma's fears were aroused, as the same man who had already been keeping an eye on her for several months "happened" to be in both offices—that of the director of the courses, she was attending, and of the chief of the militia department.

These details came to her mind a little later. After the young girl's unsuccessful attempts to get her residential permit prolonged she boarded the Sortavala train the next day and was arrested at the first little railway station during the current mandatory passport control. (Sortavala was a border region town to which one had to have a special permit or be a permanent resident). Her papers were not in order: her residential permit was no longer in force.

A small car with the same stranger in it was waiting. Thelma was shoved in and driven to the "Gray House." From then on things moved quickly. Without investigation or trial she was sentenced. She was held in the Petrozavodsk prison for seven months. To make her case look more serious the sentence was changed three times in a row: all three within the limits of Article N 58 (counter-revolution), which had by this time acquired gruesome infamy in the country. For ten long years her name was used only by ill-fated gulag inmates like herself; for the authorities she was prisoner T-572—the number sewn on her prison robes.

Ten long years of incarceration in Inta, Komi ASSR. But that was not all. The rule read that gulag inmates were not granted permission to return to their homes and families immediately upon expiration of their sentence. Another suffering was imposed on them: ten-year mandatory settlement in the same rigid northern climate. Although settlement did not imply prison walls, the situation wasn't much better. Still there was a difference—relative freedom to come and go, to work for wages, to make the best of the worst, trying to fix yourself some kind of place you could call home. Thelma threw her lot in with that of another ex-convict, a man from Latvia, Adolf Shinkis. They thought that loneliness and the trying circumstances of life were easier to overcome together. When a daughter was born to them, it was as if a ray of sunshine had broken the walls of their tedious lives, full of privations. Only Albert's curse, like that of millions of Soviets, was alcoholism, something Thelma had never observed in her better days, so she couldn't put up with it and they separated, each to go his own way.

Thelma was 42 when she and her little girl gained freedom and returned to Karelia. Mother-Elli had departed for Finland to her elderly and ailing mother. The Khrushchev "thaw" had opened a crack in the borders. Soviet citizens were beginning to travel, to see other countries and parts of the world. Thelma received an invitation from her mother to come to Finland for a visit. Sad experience told her there was no hope. How could she, a recently liberated political prisoner, get to Finland? But she was in for a great surprise on being invited to the visa department where she learned that she and daughter had been granted a month's visa. At the time she realized that there was no way for her to stay in her ancestral home: Finland had signed an agreement with the Soviet Union obliging the former to return all Soviet citizens whose visas had expired or who had illegally crossed the border. Knowing this Thelma applied to the Swedish government for political asylum. It was quickly granted.

For over twenty years Thelma has now been a happy and thriving Swedish citizen. Her daughter married and has two children. They live in the suburbs of Stockholm and see a lot of each other. Not so long ago mother and daughter visited Latvia to pay their last respects to Adolf who had succumbed to illnesses picked up in the gulag.

Exchanging letters with Thelma, talking with her on the phone was fun. It was natural to invite her to visit Karelia. She really wanted to see her former camp inmates, little Nastya and family, to get to know me personally. But was it a wonder that she hadn't rid herself of fear? Was it a wonder that the thought of safety kept gnawing at her heart?

She overcame her apprehensions and it was a delight to see this lovely lady seated in my favorite armchair, to talk with her deep into the night, to talk about our homeland that she hadn't seen since infancy, about lost opportunities (Thelma had a beautiful voice). There were many wonderful things I had to tell her. Now our exchanges have become lively and we're looking forward to seeing each other again!

THE FATE OF AN ESCAPEE

Several reasons compelled me to write in greater detail about the Abel and Sophia Janhunen family, who lived on Sumner Ave 2510, Hoaquim, Aberdeen, Washington. First, they were one of the numerous families that did not come to Karelia driven by unemployment. They had a house of their own and were comfortably off. They even paid the trip to Russia for six people who had no means of their own to pay for the crossing. Back

The Janhunen Family. Hoaquim, Washington, 1930

home father Abel was a college graduate, an experienced cabinet-maker and he felt sure that his expertise could be turned to account in the young state of workers and peasants that had recently embarked on an independent road of development. To his mind the timber trade experience in export that he had acquired at a Hoaquim sawmill, would come in handy in Russia. Upon arriving there he immediately set himself the task of learning Russian, as he didn't intend to remain in Matrosa or in the Karelles (Karelian timber) company. His dream was to work in a major port where specialists are always in demand.

Second, three gifted children, who, at the time were already asking themselves what the future had in store for them. The opportunities created by the passionate words of communist recruiters and fertile childish imagination allowed them to see themselves as prospering engineers, constructors, flyers, teachers and whatever.

Mothers are mothers. Only they, concerned with the welfare of their progeny, weigh the pros and cons and try to find that solution to the problem which would best benefit their children. Sophia Janhunen was just of the sort. She never rushed into things blindfolded, her thinking was rational and apprehensible. But try as she would she couldn't have her way. On the one hand, Abel, a devotee to the socialist Utopian ideals that governed hundreds of Finns, was bent on going to Russia. On the other hand, three kids, excited by the romantic idea of going to a mysterious far-away land, got the better of her and she finally gave in, but a sense of justified restlessness never abandoned her.

Third, the sad fate of the Janhunen family mirrors that of hundreds of others but it has striking nuances of its own, connected with the illness and loss of Abel on April 14, 1932, and the vicissitudes of the sons Allan, the eldest, and Paul.

The Janhunens enjoyed US insurance Abel had provided for them, so they had no financial troubles. Soon their paths crossed with Pekka Saastamoinen, a political emigrant from Finland. His heart was warmed by the cordial relations in the Janhunen family. Pekka was quite desolate and distressed himself, as his wife and three children lived in Finland and refused to join him in Karelia, which he, in turn, was ideologically committed to. It didn't take long for Pekka to become husband to Sophia and father to the children, who considered themselves fortunate to now have a family head and breadwinner. The word stepfather has the same concealed negative connotation in every language and that explains why the three children never spoke of Pekka as their stepfather, he was Father. But Abel's memory was kept evergreen by every family member.

Saying farewell to the Janhunens. Aberdeen, Washington, October, 1931

Saastamoinen was a qualified and highly respected worker at the prewar Petrozavodsk ski factory. The family welfare was always his immediate concern, so in no time the Janhunens joined the "Valuta" cooperative engaged in building houses for immigrants from America. ("Valuta" means foreign currency. All the building materials and labor were paid for in US dollars.) Before this house was completed you could find Pekka on the opposite shore of the Petrozavodsk Bay chopping away at logs for a summer house. The Ski factory had just been granted a lot for its workers to put up "dachas," as they are called in Russia, and Pekka was among the first to jump at the idea. This

Irma Sazonova and Allan Jahunen; sister and brother.

dacha area went up quickly and it was the first of its kind to appear in Karelia, thanks to the initiative displayed by the then-director of the Ski factory Tuomainen, a highly regarded organizer of production from Finland, who was paid in the same coin—prison.

The grim year of 1937 found the family comfortably established: Irma, the youngest, and Paul were going to school; in the summer of 1937 Allan graduated a two-year Finnish language course at the local Teachers' College. He got a teaching position at the Rukajärvi high school and was happy with it. The purges were already underway but the Janhunen-Saastamoinen family remained unscathed. No one had the slightest premonition of the trials that awaited them. The blows began falling one by one.

The summer of 1938 saw the inexplicable arrests of numerous American youngsters, 19-year-old Paul among them. Dragged away by the NKVD on July 11, 1938, he was executed on September 24, the same year, only this became known 55 years later! A definite pattern could be observed: arrests triggered off another manifestation of illegality—evictions and exiles. Militia officials had taken a fancy to the so-called Valuta house, so small wonder that families in which someone had been arrested, were among the first to be thrown out of their homes and dachas. Very soon this house acquired a new name: the Militia house: they were the people who replaced the lawful tenants.

The place of exile where the Janhunens landed as members of an-enemy-of-the-people family was Yandoma, a small settlement to the south of Petrozavodsk on the Svirj River. Allan had been put out of his teaching job, as by that time Finnish was proclaimed a bourgeois language and struck off the curriculum, so he joined the family and once again they were united, but this time without the youngest son Paul.

Another Finnish-American family that was in Yandoma were mother and son Maria and Arnold Pilppola. No available information on the father—Nestor Pilppola. So, putting two and two together (families of-enemies-of-the-people), it's not hard to imagine what had happened to him.

Little by little people began receiving permission to return to Petrozavodsk. April 1939 found the family in town, searching for a place to live. There was no returning to the apartment nor to the dacha that legally belonged to them. They were shooed off and told to forget it. But the ski factory was eager to get Pekka back: his reputation was stainless and qualifications high. This factory, like many others, was short of hands. (A Petrozavodsk newspaper has published a Martyrologue which includes 40 names of victims, five Finnish-Americans among them. The list is incomplete. See appendixes). But all they could offer for living quarters was one room in an old dilapidated house on Bolotnaya Street. Beggars aren't choosers: the whole family just had to squeeze in.

The predatory wars of 1939 didn't spare Finnish-American families either. Allan was drafted into the so-called National Army but survived as he never was in action. He was still in military service in the vicinity of Aunus when war broke out in 1941. The family, like all others in Petrozavodsk, was evacuated and ever since then they knew nothing of Allan's fate. The first time that any news came to their ears was in 1974 when, through relatives in Finland, they learned that Allan had been taken prisoner by the Finland army and, upon getting a chance to escape to Sweden, he had crossed the border and handed himself over to Swedish authorities. As an American-born he was immediately granted asylum. Allan related to his sister a funny incident that had occurred at the border. The presiding officer greeted him with the words, "Welcome! Your sister arrived in Sweden a few weeks ago. She also was a POW in Finland." This "mystery" was cleared up later when Irma established direct contact with Allan. We now know that this "sister" was another lady who happily reached her homeland and is now comfortably enjoying old age at Home.

Two escapees. Unto Kainu (left) and Allan Janhunen. Sweden, 1945.

Allan didn't make the escape alone. Another young American from Petrozavodsk,

Unto Kainu, accompanied him. These two were not the only ones, but for reasons understood, I shall not mention other names but only express the hope that they are living, enjoying good health and freedom. The reader is already aware of the sad fate that awaited those who were forcibly returned.

Allan and Unto soon married Swedish girls. Unto's life was not so eventful, up to his dying day he lived in Sweden.

The sufferings and trials endured by Allan were numerous and they did not go unnoticed. Three years of captivity in Finland—interrogations, including a faked execution by a firing squad in the forest, meager rations, escape—everything had left an indelible trace. Allan couldn't bear the closeness of Finland—Russia was too near. He feared the day would come when he'd be forcefully returned to Russia. Fear! Fear! Fear became a permanent concomitant he couldn't rid himself of up to his last breath!

Allan's homeland, the USA, kept calling. He couldn't resist the temptation and soon left for his native state of Washington with his wife. Probably there, he thought, he'd feel at ease; he wouldn't always have to look over his shoulder to see whether someone wasn't keeping an eye on him.

Little by little, with the help of good friends, they got started. Two sons were born to them in the US. The first thing Allan did was to build a house. To make money for the family he sold it and began putting up a new one. Throughout their stay in the US Allan felt he was being tailed but he wasn't sure; he ascribed this sense of suspicion to his former fears born in Fin-

Abel Janhunen, manager, in the lumberyard. Hoaquim, Washington, 1928

land and Sweden. But nothing doing! The second house wasn't even finished when he was arrested, accused of false identity and espionage in favor of the USSR. McCarthyism was just surfacing in the US: numerous anti-communist processes, especially in the world of art were underway; fear and suspicion were being instilled in a freedom-loving nation. And just look! Here's a blood-in-the-flesh Soviet spy walking into the hands of the secret police! Once again Allan was subjected to the cruelty of incarceration, but this time he found himself in a mental institution: interrogations by psychologists and psychiatrists, injections, threats. His health was completely broken. Listening to Irma's narration of Allan's sufferings, I relived the disturbing horrors of "One Flew Over the Cuckoo's Nest." Only this time the victim was one of us and his tragic life story is coming to the reader thanks to his sister.

Allan's childhood friends, who had accorded the family a warm welcome, didn't leave them in the lurch. Lawyers were hired and soon came the day justice triumphed. Allan's two sons Gary and Paul were already attending an American school. His wife felt so harrassed that she refused to spend another day in America, and soon the family returned to Sweden, where Irma visited with them several times.

But even here in serene and peaceful Sweden life wasn't all smooth sailing. The family knew no economic difficulties: money Allan had earned in the States, the pension he received from the US government, school grants and discounts generously provided by the Swedish government enabled the family to have a nice home and saw to all their needs. But Allan was unwell: the mania of persecution kept intensifying and there was no way to rid him of the idea that his every step was under constant surveillance. It was many a time that he was taken to hospital for medical treatment and in the latter years he even refused to receive guests without having previously seen their photos, so that he himself could establish their identity: fear was overwhelming.

It's a pity Allan never finished the book he had begun writing: we'd have a deeper insight into the workings of his mind, into the sufferings he had unrightfully been subjected to. There's a limit to one's endurance! The day came when Dr. Death came knocking at his door to bring him relief. That was in 1992.

During the war years Sophia, Pekka and Irma were evacuated from Karelia to Nyandoma, the Arkhangel region, and from there back to Karelia, to Tchupa in the north. The hardships evacuees endured were hard on the elderly and especially men: Pekka's last resting place is in Tchupa, Sophia died in 1947 in Petrozavodsk. Irma is still going strong. Even after retirement she goes on leading an active life, which includes a lot of travelling. Every other year she visited Allan until he passed on. Finland remains her favorite leisure spot. And, of course, her two sons and their children are a consolation.

A few months ago Irma was in for a pleasant surprise. The present-day Russian government has adopted measures to make amends for the illegal confiscation of property of purge victim families. They get discounts in the constantly mounting rent and public utility charges. Luckily Irma had saved the papers proving that all the building expenses in the "Valuta" house, where they had lived up to eviction, had been paid in dollars. Thus the reimbursment was unexpected and substantial. Here's hoping it will allow Irma to live a long life in dignified style and keep up the travelling.

TONMEISTER

"Tonmeister," the German word for "sound engineer," is how Petrozavodsk TV producer Lartseva entitled her article honoring Elmer Nousiainen on his jubilee in April. "Sound" is a wonderful word to characterize Elmer. He's sound in every respect: he has a sound music ear, he's a sound husband, father, friend and employee, he makes sound judgements. Seeing this soft-spoken smiling man, who doesn't look his age, you'd take him for the happiest guy on earth, for one whom worldly troubles had never visited. But that's not so: he's had his share of the Stalinist trials but he hasn't let them pull him down.

Elmer was a high school student in Daisytown, Pennsylvania, when his father, a miner put on the dole, and mother sold their home, packed their belongings and set off on the same fateful voyage as thousands of others idealistic Finns from America. Elmer's most cherished treasure was his saxophone and that's what he carried, never parting with it. If the sax could talk, it'd have quite a story to tell.

First the family went to Kuzbass but John Nousiainen's health was failing so they left for Karelia where they settled down in Petrozavodsk. At the time another American Theodore Hautala was setting up the long-distance radio station and he was happy to get such a reliable assistant as Elmer. There was a third American working with them, Donald Närväinen from Minnesota, who, by the way, retired from the post of chief engineer of Karelian Radio and TV shortly before his demise. Hautala, Närväinen and Nousiainen made quite a team and soon the town had a radio station of its own. It can be regarded as one of the numerous monuments Finnish-Americans left behind.

Some things haven't been lost track of. Lartseva recalls an interesting episode from Elmer's radio days. People complained of poor reception. Elmer thought he'd see what could be done about it. His professional knowledge told him a transformer was needed. But he had to have 10 kg of metal to make the core. No metal to be had. With the help of neighbors and friends Elmer started collecting used tin cans and it didn't take him long to make the amplifier. Radio reception was excellent.

Peaceful work was interrupted by the state policy of persecution: the banning of the Finnish language and all its institutions, the purges and the lay-offs of foreigners holding decent jobs. One day, when Elmer came to work, he was turned back and told he'd been discharged as they were "cutting down on personnel". His sax was lying in its case appealing to him, "Let's go job-hunting together". And so they did. Elmer's first job as a musician was in a local band, where he acquired the professionalism which he didn't even dream would come in so handy in future.

With things going on the way they were (arrests were in full swing, Theodore Hautala was arrested in 1937) Elmer made up his mind to return to his homeland. 1938. Only a few hours had passed after his leaving the US Embassy in Moscow when he was nabbed and accused of "being suspected of espionage," Thus began the eight years of his gulag experiences. His logging career was happily cut short: once again the sax intervened. They were putting together an "amateur" art brigade in the prison camp. Amateur stands in brackets because the whole lot was made up of professionals from the Bolshoi and Kiev opera theaters. A highly distinguished and popular Estonian singer Ants Eskola was among them. In camps Elmer actually got to understand the international character of Marx's "Workers of the world, unite!" the art brigade united people speaking 13 languages.

Sixteen years passed before Elmer managed to return home. First music preoccupied him. He played in a jazz orchestra and then in the symphony. But technically-minded as he was Donald Närväinen talked him into returning to sound engineering.

We often hear "They are made for each other". That certainly applies to Elmer and his wife Miriam who is "the last of the Vermonters." Her story is very much like Elmer's, only their family was spared the gulags. Miriam and family, father, mother and younger sister, arrived in Petrozavodsk from Vermont in 1934. The David and Lydia Hasko family from Bondville, Vermont had nothing to gain but a well-provided for life to lose. To her dying day Lydia Haasko couldn't forgive herself for the pressure she had put on her husband to join the people leaving for Karelia. By 1934 many had already returned and they had bitter experiences to render but Lydia refused to believe them.

Life in Russia had hardships in store for one and all. If nothing else, at least the living conditions and then WWII with evacuation to hunger-stricken areas like the White Sea port of Arkhangelsk. Miriam considers them lucky to have landed a job at a dried vegetable factory. Knibbling at a carrot, beet and even an onion was what kept them alive and made it possible for them to return to their devastated homes in 1944. Miriam recalls the first day of their work at the factory. She wasn't coping with the quota, so Mother came to her help. Wasn't the manager surprised and proud announcing to the other workers that these two new-comers had fulfilled the quota on the very first day. No wonder! Working ethics are instilled in Finns from childhood.

Miriam and Elmer Nousiainen, June 1994, Townshend, VT.

Miriam was only a schoolgirl at the time but she didn't go to the school the first year as it was miles away and no transport. But the next year she took up her studies in the eighth grade walking all the way there on Monday and back on Friday. The students feared nothing more than a possible onslaught of hungry wolves. Miriam recalls how she always carried dry sticks and matches in case of emergency.

Hard worker that she was Miriam lost no time in getting an education to qualify for her teaching English. Thus she worked her way through night school and college and became a highly qualified teacher and then vice-principal of school N 17, where the students major in English. She was very ingenious and up to this day her colleagues remember innovations introduced by Mira Stepanovna, as she was affectionately called.

The Nousiainens and Haaskos were friends in prewar Karelia but the 10-year difference in Elmer's and Miriam's age prevented them from getting closer at the time. When Elmer returned after his forced wanderings, they didn't find each other at once as they lived in different towns—Miriam in Sortavala and Elmer in Petrozavodsk. Five years passed before she took a group of students on a field trip to the radio station where they had an excellent English-speaking guide, Elmer Nousiainen. Thanks to this event they began seeing a lot of each other, married soon and became a happy couple.

Lydia passed away. Cisko, the younger sister was married and had two daughters but merciless cancer struck and the two girls' father agreed to Elmer's and Miriam's becoming their parents with all the ensuing obligations. People who know nothing about the actual state of affairs have no idea that Elmer and Miriam are not the biological parents. Not every daughter and grandchild gets all the loving care and attention that is theirs.

A natural yearning to see the home parts never left the Nousiainens. They have now retrieved their American citizenship and have paid two visits to Vermont. During the second visit Elmer and Miriam also spent a few days in Pennsylvania. How exciting it was for both of them to find their homes, relatives, Miriam's nonagenarian aunt Eva Jones among them, and former schoolmates. Miriam was deeply moved by Vermont Governor Dean's reception and the plaque he extended certifying that she has been conferred title of Honorary Citizen of Vermont.

Vermont and Karelia are closely connected today. Since Governor Madelaine Kunin's first visit to Petrozavodsk in 1989 great things have been happening. I had the opportunity and great pleasure of learning a lot from my highly esteemed Vermont friends Supreme Court Judge John Dooley, Bar Association lawyers Jan Eastman and John Marshall, Judge Amy Davenport and lawyer Mark Ottinger, who simply charmed the Law school students of Petrozavodsk Unversity during his stay as Fullbright professor, and many, many others. Their unstinted efforts to put the badly-needed "Rule of Law" project into effect in Russian is highly appreciated by their Karelian colleagues and the public at large.

Miriam and Elmer Nousiainen are extremely active Russia-United States citizens. They have become contact persons for Project Harmony from Waitsville, Vermont. Project Harmony, organized and directed by father and son Charles and David Hosford, has wrought useful changes in mutual relations. Exchanges organized by them involve teachers and students, musicians and artists, firefighters and police. There's no unit to measure the advantages and benefit of these exchanges, probably only the grateful hearts and new-born mutual understanding on both sides of the ocean.

1996 is an eventful year for both Miriam and Elmer, the year in which they are celebrating their 70th and 80th birthdays respectively. Surely all my readers will join in wishing them a long and happy life, productive "dacha" seasons, success for the girls and more eventful visits to their homeland.

Be happy, dear friends!

9 Lest We Forget.

AFTERWORD

Memory is short. The passing of time is swift.

It's rightfully considered that each experience should benefit the people involved, the society they belonged to and, in the long run, humanity. This could happen only if memory were sustained and we'd all learn to distinguish good from the bad, to nurture and expand the good, to eliminate and destroy the bad.

Is this happening? No!

Pleasant memories have long lives. There's a tendency to forget the tragedies and miseries of the past. Moreover we constantly witness attempts on behalf of ambitious self-seeking politicians to intentionally wipe out crimes that have cost innocent human lives.

1917–1996—almost 90 years! Was the "socialist" Revolution in Russia a success? No! The price the people paid—millions of lives—substantially outweighs the good.

Has the failure of communism in Russia and in the world taught mankind a lesson? No! Communists are not only abiding time, they are actively staging a comeback. In Russia they are taking advantage of the poverty-stricken population's natural aspirations for bread. The corruption-riddled government and bureaucracy took its lessons from the communist leaders whose portraits are once again in the hands of supporters. The bloody past is forgotten and Zyuganov has been heard to say that Stalin wasn't so bad.

The 1917 Revolution poured water on the mill of radicals throughout the world. Waves of well-wishers from numerous countries went to Russia to help with their expertise, personal means and good will. Dealing with numbers Germans are the runners-up: 650. Finnish-Americans take the lead: 5,596. Their emigration from the USA and Canada was a unique organized experience, the tragic aftermath of which is the following:

Out of the total 5,596 arrivals, 1,346 returned. Not all the remaining can be accounted for. Nothing is known of the fate of 950.

Taking all the historical events into account: the purges, warfare, evacuation into distant parts of the USSR, and natural deaths it will evidently never be possible to establish what and when exactly happened to each immigrant, although, hopefully, the number of returnees to the West is larger than the recorded 1,346.

Of the accountable 3,300 the following has been established:

the total number of purge victims	853

Differentiation by countries:	
from the USA	533
from Canada	312
Questionable	8

Differentiation by gender:	
men	790
women	63

Out of the total 590 have been rehabilitated. Not a single case is known to have been turned down as not eligible for rehabilitation. The total does not include Finnish-Americans whom colleagues claim to have disappeared during the purges, but no official record has been found *(62).*

Up to 1933 the Resettling Management kept count of natural deaths of immigrants *(77).*

Perished in war or are among the missing *(109)*

This figure does nor include a number of men whose deaths have not been documented, i.e. Wäinö Rimpinen (from New York), Wäinö Heimola (Detroit), Aarne Wiitanen (Waukegan Ill.) and others.

War-time labor camps also took a high toll of Finnish-Americans (see App. 5) *(61)*

LC victims who returned to their families	*60*
Victims of the Leningrad siege	*13*
Total of victimized Finnish-Americans	*1,235*

We cannot disregard the sufferings heaped on families that lost their breadwinners—fathers and/or mothers, sons and daughters, brothers and sisters. Not all of them survived either.

With the present-day development of events in Russia it wouldn't be an overstatement to say that never, never will the millions of Russian victims of communism be remembered by monuments erected to them. The number of those who WANT to forget is growing.

If only the victims of Lenin, Stalin and Hitler, Mao and Ceaucescu, Pol Pot and Castro and other tyrants could rise from their graves and tell their stories, no vestiges of communism would remain on earth!

In this light the 1993 decision of the US government, authorizing a memorial to the victims of communism, deserves the highest appreciation. Undoubtedly Americans and people of goodwill throughout the world will do their bit to raise the required 100 million dollars. We and generations to come must not forget!

Mankind has other enemies: avarice, greed and avidity. These spark off upheavals and crimes. Life tends to prove that this phenomenon does not belong to a certain –ism; it's an individual feature, but it's manifest everywhere and at all times. There's no way to measure the misery it wroughts.

Time and again our thoughts turn to the political philosophy of our elders and we ponder over the similarity of our upbringing as compared to that of church-goers which we were not. "Thou shall not covet" was one of the guiding principals. And we've lived accordingly.

Bringing this life mission to completion I'm sorry not to experience a greater sense of satisfaction: so many questions remain, so many people have not been found, there are so many discrepancies. There's no way to rid myself of the pain and sadness caused by the senseless losses My People have borne but there's also hope. Hope that common sense will prevail in the world. Hope that generations of our offspring will draw conclusions from the lives of their parents, grandparents and greatgrandparents. Hope that the destructive forces of communism will never again lead people astray or produce tyrants. Hope that greed and avidity will never prosper.

LITERATURE

1. Andriainen Antti. NEUVOSTO-KARJALAA AVUSTAMASSA. /Helping Soviet Karelia/, "Carelia", 1993/2. Petrozavodsk.
2. Sevander Mayme with Laurie Hertzel. THEY TOOK MY FATHER. Pfeifer-Hamilton Publisher, Duluth, 1992.
3. Sevander Mayme. RED EXODUS. Oscat publishers with Atlas Games. Duluth, MN., 1993.
4. Volkogonov Dmitri. LENIN. POLITICHESKY PORTRET. V DVUKH KNIGAH. /Lenin. Political portrait, In two books/. Novosti, Moscow, 1994.
5. Radzinsky Edward. STALIN. Doubleday New York, 1996.
6. Vaksberg Arkdij. HERRAR OCH LAKEJER. Ur Kominterns Hemliga Historia. /Masters and Lackeys. On Comintern's dreadful history/. Norstedts (Sweden), 1995.
7. Singer Daniel. THE FUTURE OF SOCIALISM. "Against the Current", # 51, Detroit, MI.
8. "Red Exodus", quote 56 on p.144.
9. Kero Reino, "Red Exodus," p.p.41–42.
10. Ibid. Quoted in "Red Exodus", p.39.
11. "Red Exodus" p.p.54–66.
12. Finnish-language journals "Carelia" published in Petrozavodsk. 1991 (1–12), 1992 (1–6).
13. Freemantle Brian. KGB. New York Holt, Rinehart and Winston, 1982.
14. Takala Irja. V POISKAKH ELDORADO. SEVERO-AMERIKIANSKIE FINNY V DOVOENNOI KARELII. /Searching for Eldorado. North-American Finns in Pre-War Karelia./ and REPRESSIVNAYA POLITIKA V OTNOSHENII FINNOV V SOVETSKOI KARELII 30-KH GODOV. /A Policy of Repression towards Finns in Soviet Karelia in the Thirties/. Both published in the journal "Voprosy Istorii Yevropeiskovo Severa" /Problems on the History of the European North/, published by Petrozavodsk University, 1993.
15. KHRUSHCHEV REMEMBERS with an Introduction, Commentary and Notes by Edward Crankshaw. Little, Brown and Company. Boston and Toronto, 1970, p.p.152–155.
16. Engle Eloise and Paananen Lauri. THE WINTER WAR. THE SOVIET ATTACK ON FINLAND 1939–1940. Stackpole Books. 1973.
17. VECHNAYA SLAVA GEROYAM. /Eternal Glory to Heroes/. Carelia publishers, 1992. Petrozavodsk.

18. KNIGA PAMYATI, /Book of Memory/. Carelia publishers, 1944. Petrozavodsk.

19. Gilbert Martin. ATLAS OF RUSSIAN HISTORY. 1984. Dorset Press, p.9: Labour Camps in European Russia, 1917–1936.

20. Map from WINTER WAR, p.17 "The Concentration of Russian Divisions against Finland in November 1939".

21. KRA documents. They all fall under files NN 685, 190.

22. NKVDA documents are differentiated in the text: files, Albums and Protocols.

23. The Finland Military files bear NN 19658, 19661, 19662 and T-8449, T-6863/26, T-68631, 4902/51, T-19653/56, T-19653/78, T-19658/13-15, T-19653/9-10.

APPENDIXES

APPENDIX 1.

Victims of Stalinism rehabilitated in keeping with presentations of security organs and "memorial" society.

Lists published in the journal "Carelia."

(NB: indication of year of death as 1937 or 1938 comes from the NKVDA file and apparently implies execution. Not all the names are to be found in Protocols. In the fraction the numerator indicates the year, the denominator—the N of the issue. The name of a province in Finland has the letter "l", meaning "lääni", attached to it: Porinl.—the Pori province; the "p", attached to a following name, means "pitäjä": Raumanp—the district of Rauma; "k"—"kylä" means village. Most of this information is lacking and will hopefully be supplied by readers).

AALTIO Arvid, b. 1892, from US in 1931, Petrozavodsk, ski factory, 91/1—a 10-year sentence.

AALTIO Toimi, 1913–1938, b. US; from US in 1931; Vilga, logger; 91/1.

AALTO Jalmar,1890–1938; b. Finland, Turku-Porinl., from US in 1932; Petrozavodsk, driver; 91/1.

AALTONEN Mauno, 1904–38, b. Finland, Turunl.; from Canada 1932; Matrosa, logger; 91/1.

AHO Kusti (Kalle), 1889–1938. b. Oulunl., Pyhäkoski; from US in 1931; Kondopoga construction; 91/1.

AHOLA Leonard, 1903–37; from US 1931; Rugozero, logging manager; 91/1.

AHTI Jukka, 1897–38; b. Finland, Kotka; from US 1931; Petrozavodsk, Onega plant; 91/4. His wife LAMMI Katri was also arrested, but she returned (See "R.E.", p.110)

ALAKATILA August, 1896–1938, b. Oulunl. Järvenkylä; from Canada 1932; Segezha district, Losinaya Gora, logger; 91/1.

ALHAINEN Niilo, 1896–1937; from Canada 1933; Prionezhye district, Interposyolok, logger; 91/1.

ALHAINEN (Lokasaari) Lilly, wife of Niilo. In his papers the arrest of his wife is indicated, although there are no separate documents.

ANDERSON Antti, 1878–1940. b. Oulunl., Ankkala; from Canada 1932; Kondopoga, Sunastroi; 91/1.

ANDERSON Evert, 1889–1937; b. Finland, from Canada 1932, arr.in Leningrad; 91/2.

ANDERSON Olga 1890–1932; b. Finland; from Canada 1932; arr. in Leningrad; 91/4.

ANDERSON Olavi (Evert's son), 1914–32; arr. in Leningrad; 91/4.

ANDERSON Tauno,1916–1938. b. US, Ashtabula, Ohio; Repola, machine operator; 91/1.

ANTTILA Jalmari, 1900–1938, b. Finland; Kondopoga paper mill worker; 91/1.

ARKILANDER Antti, 1889–1938, b. Finland; from US; 91/1.

ARKILANDER Werner (son of Antti), 1914–1938, b. US; Kondopoga paper mill, driver; 91/1.

BACKMAN August (Kustaa), 1891–1938; b. Finland, Kuhmo, from US 1932; Uhtua, worker; 91/1.

BJÖRKLUND Adolf, 1878–1938; b. Vaasanl., Pulkkila, from US 1932; Uhtua; 91/2.

BROMSI Juho (John), 1907–1937; b. Finland; from Canada 1933; Petrozavodsk, Karelles; 91/2.

DAHLMAN Kauko; 1918–1938, b. US; from US 1932; Kondopoga logging, driver; 91/3.

DAVIDSON Jack, 1889–38, b. Oulunl., Tykkä; from Rock, Mich. 1932; Suurjärvi, Muyezersk district, locomotive driver; 91/3.

EKHOLM Arvid, 1908–38, b. Uudenmaanl. Oskarinp.; from Baltimore, Maryland in 1931; Padany, Segezha district. assistant director of an enterprise; 92/3.

EKLIN Matti, 1880–1938; B. Vaasanl., Jyväskoskenp.; from US 1932; Petrozavodsk, laborer; 92/6.

EKLIN Heino, 1890–38; b. Finland; not exactly known where he is from; Solomennoye, worker; 91/6.

ELO Kerttu (Hertta), 1901–1938; b. Helsinki; from US 1934; Petrozavodsk, ski factory; 92/3.

ERKKILÄ Harold, 1904–38; b. Vaasanl. Keskikylä; from Canada 1932;

ESKELINEN Tahvo, 1900–1938; b. F.Kuopionl., Pajusenmäki; from Matrosa, logger; 92/3.

ESKOLA Eino, 1917, b. US, US citizen; Petrozavodsk; 92/3 a 3-year sentence.

ESKOLA Samuel, 1882–1937, b. Vaasa, from US 1931; Interposyolok, driver; 92/3.

FILPUS Elvira, 1888–1938; b. Orinmatinl, Huhta; from US 1933; Petrozavodsk, homemaker; 92/3.

FILPUS Niilo, 1880–1938, b. Finland; from US in 1933; Petrozavodsk; 92//3.

GOLBERG Olavi, 1917–1938, b. US, Alaska,from US in 1931; Uhtua, worker; 91/3.

GRÖNLUND Frans-Jalmari, 1893–1938; b. Finland, from Canada 1932; arr. in Leningrad; 91/4.

GRÖNROOS Lauri, 1905–1938; b. F., from US 1932; Kondopoga,

Lenlesstroi; 91/3.

HAAKANA Antti, 1903–1938, b. Viipurinl.; from Canada 1932; Segezha district, Losinaya Gora logger; 92/3.

HAAPALAINEN Toivo, 1912–1938, b. Helsinki, from US in 1922; Petrozavodsk ski factory; 91/9.

HAAPANIEMI Sylvester, 1905–1938; b. Finland; from US 1932; Kondopoga; 92/3.

HAAPANEN Eero, 1895–?; b. Finland; from Canada in 1932; Belomorsk district, Kolezhma; 92/3—a 7-year sentence.

HAAPASAARI Matti, 1905–1938; b. Finland; from US 1931; Petrozavodsk, Onega plant worker; 92/3.

HAAVIO Kaarlo (Kalle), b. Finland; from Ludlow, Vermont 1933; Uhtua, logger; 92/3.

HAHTI Martti, 1913–?; b. Turku; from US 1932; Karelavto, driver; 91/3, a 10-year sentence.

HAKA Kalle, 1901–?, b. Finland; from US; Petrozavodsk, editor of Finnish newspaper; 92/3.

HAKALA Arthur, 1889–1938; b. Finland Sormarinp., Sormari; from Canada 1932; Kondopoga district, Sandal logging camp; 92/3; no info on American-born (1925) son George.

HAKKARAINEN August, 1901–1937; b. Finland; from US in 1932; Sandal logging camp; 92/3.

HALBERG (Hagberg)Iisak, 1889–1938; b. Finland, Rovaniemi; from US; Rukajärvi, logger; 92/3.

HALME Iivari, 1885–1938; b. Turunl., Kilnakkola; from Newberry, Mich.; Prionezhye district, logger; 92/3.

HALMELA Wäinö, 1888–1938; b. Vaasanl., Närtiö; from US 1932; Uhtua, carpenter; 92/3.

HÄMÄLÄINEN Eino, 1912–?; b. Hibbing, Minn.; from US 1931; Petrozavodsk brick factory; 92/3—a 10-year sentence.

HÄMÄLÄINEN Matti, 1897–1938; b. Finland, Vastinga; from Canada, 1932; Vilga, logger; 92/3.

HÄMÄLÄINEN Yrjö, 1889–? (no sentence indicated), b. Finland, 1932 from Waukegan, Ill.; Pudozh district, logger; 92/3.

HANHISALO Aune-ILmari, 1908–1938; b. Vaasanl. from Canada; Matrosa, logger; 92/3.

HARHIO August-Werner, 1879–?; b. Finland, from South Dakota 1931; Aunus district, agriculture laborer; 92/3—a 5-year sentence.

HARJU Tuomas, 1910–1938; b. Vaasanl., Keura; from Canada 1931; Petrozavodsk ski factory; 92/3.

HARJU Yrjö,1916–?, b. Canada; Matrosa, logger; 92/3—a 5-year sentence.

HASALA Hilja, 1898–1938; b. Finland; from Myrtle Lake, Minn.; Vilga; 92/3.

HASALA Wilho, 1918–1938, b. US, Virginia, Minn., from US; Padozero, logger; 92/3.

HAUTALA Antti, 1899–1938; b. Finland; Petrozavodsk lumber yard; 92/3.

HEIKKILÄ Wäinö, 1885–1938; b. Oulunl., Kestilä, from Canada 1931; Rugozero, logger; 92/3.

HEIKKINEN Arvo, 1911–1938, b. Canada, Fort William; from Canada 1932; Petrozavodsk, driver; 92/3.

HEIKKINEN Tauno, 1915–38, b. Canada, from Canada 1932; Matrosa, logger; 92/3.

HEIKKINEN Victor 1898–?; b. Viipuri; from Canada 1931; Petrozavodsk, Karelavto; 92/3—a 3-year sentence.

HEIMONEN Edward, 1887–1938; b. Kuopionl., Kirkko, from US 1931; Petrozavodsk construction; 92/3.

HEINO Albin, 1885–1938; b. Finland; from Sugar Isl., Mich.1931; Petrozavodsk ski factory; 92/3.

HEINO (Heinonen) Eino, 1910–1938; b. ?; from US 1931; Kondopoga paper mill; 92/3.

HEINO Frank, 1887–38; b. Finland, from Menagha, Minn.; Kondopoga paper mill; 92/3.

HEINO Frans, 1876–1938, b. Finland, Petälänkylä; from US in 1922; Petrozavodsk ski factory; 92/2.

HELA Daniel, 1874–1938, b. Viipurinl., Emmanp.; from Canada 1932; Petrozavodsk ski factory; 92/3.

HELA Eero, 1913–38, b. US, from Canada 1932; Uhtua district, technician in logging; 92/3.

HELANDER Yrjö-Niilo, 1899–38; b. Finland; from US in 1932; Petrozavodsk construction; 92/3.

HELANDER Wäinö, 1896–1938, b. Finland, from US in 1931; Kondopoga, Sunastroi; 92/3;

HELIN Wilho, 1898–1938; b. Finland, Uudenmaanl., Mäntylä; came from US; Kondopoga paper mill; 92/3.

HENDRICKSON Alexander-Axel, 1893–1938, b. Finland, Turunl.; from Brooklyn, NY 1932; Petrozavodsk printers; 92/3.

HENDRICKSON John, 1986–1938; b. Finland, Metsälänkartano; from US 1931; Petrozavodsk, Karelavto; 92/3.

HENELL Benjamin, 1905–1937; b. Finland; from US; Kiestinki House of Culture; 92/3.

HERNESALMI (Hernekoski) Nestor, 1900–1938; from US in 1933; Padozero, logger; 92/3.

HERRALA Erkki, 1896–1938; b. Finland; from US 1932; Solomennoye power station; 92/3.

HILL Eino, 1914–1938, b. Helsinki; from Canada 1931; Matrosa, logger; 92/3.

HILL Helen, 1917–?; b. Minn.US; from US in 1932; Uhtua, Kannussuo;

92/3—a 10-year sentence.

HILL Henrick (Heikki), 1895–38; b. Vaasanl., Kerttulank.; from Warren, Ohio, 1931; Petrozavodsk ski factory; 92/3.

HILL Victor, 1989–1938; b. Finland; from Mich.1933; Uhtua, mason; 92/3.

HILL Walfred, 1914–38, b. Canada, Montreal; from Canada 1932; Petrozavodsk ski factory; 92/3.

HINTSANEN Emil, 1898–1938; b. Finland; from Canada; Kondopoga logging center; 92/3.

HOLTTI Olavi, 1911–1938; b. Vaasa; 1932 from US; Petrozavodsk, musician; 91/9.

HONGISTO Wäinö, 1892–1938; b. Hämeenl., Ruskolank.; Lososinnoye, logger; 92/3.

HONKANEN Iivari, 1885–?; from US 1932; Kiestinki, construction worker; 92/3, a 10-year sentence.

HUHTALA Erik (Erkki), 1888–1938, b. Vaasanl.; from Canada 1931; Petrozavodsk, Onega plant; 92/3.

HUHTALA Juho, 1883–1938; b. Vaasanl., Tohonlampi; from Quincy, Mass. 1932; Prionezhye, Shoksa, quarry worker; 92/3.

HUUKI Kalle, 1898–1937; b. US; from Fairport, Ohio 1931; Interposyolok, logger; 92/3. In "Album" he's charged with having fought on the side of the White army in the Russian Civil war.

HYVÄRINEN Antti, 1885–1938; b. Finland; from Brush Prairie, Wash. in 1932; quarry worker in Kondopoga district; 92/3.

IMMONEN Arvid Viktor's son, 1912–1938; b. US, from US in 1932; Aunus, driver; 91/4.

IMMONEN Viktor, 1884–?; b. Finland, Vaukkola; from US 1925; Kiestinki, baker; 91/4—a 10-year sentence.

JÄÄSKELÄINEN Juho (John), 1884–1938; b. Kuopinol.; from US in 1934; Uhtua Kannussuo logger; 92/4.

JÄÄSKELÄINEN Matti, 1901–1938; b. Oulunl.; from Canada 1931; Kondopoga paper mill; 92/4.

JÄRVENPÄÄ Eero, 1905–1938; b. Vaasanl., Pihlaja; from US, 1931; Rugozero logger; 92/4.

JÄRVINEN Viktor, 1903–1938; b. Vaasanl.; from Canada 1932; Kiestinki, constructor; 92/4.

JUNTUNEN Aarne 1914–1938, b. Finland; from Canada 1932; Padozero, logger; 92/4.

JUNTUNEN Otto 1911–1938 (brother of Aarne); b. Finland, from Canada in 1932; (in "Album").

JUNTUNEN Kaarlo, 1893–1938; b. Finland; from Canada 1931; Uhtua agriculture laborer; 92/4.

JURVA Otto, 1895–1938, b. Finland; from Calumet, Mich. US 1931; Kolatselkä, agronomist; 92/4.

JURVANEN Kalle, 1905–1938; b. Finland, Sortavala; from Canada 1931; Lososinnoye camp logger; 92/4.

JUUTILAINEN Oskari, 1899–1938; b. Kotka; from US in 1932; Petrozavodsk ski factory; 92/4.

JUVONEN Juho, 1887–1938; b. Viipurinl., Riisko; Petrozavodsk ski factory; 92/4.

JUVONEN Uuno, 1900–1938; b. F.Viipurinl., Ruokorannank.; from US 1931; Kondopoga construction; 92/4.

KÄÄNTÖ Yrjö, 1900–1938; b. Finland, Kalajoki; from Canada in 1931 (?); Matrosa, logger; 91/6.

KAIPAINEN Juho, 1887–1938, b. Finland and wife

KAIPAINEN Maria 1890–1938, b. Finland, both from Buffalo, NY, 1932; Kondopoga, construction workers; 91/4.

KALLILA Helen-Melisse, 1919–1938; b. Turun-Porinl., Salonk.; from US 1932; Petrozavodsk, music school student; 91/5.

KALLIO Julius, 1891–1938, b. Finland; from US 1931; Petrozavodsk, Finnish National theater, producer; 91/5.

KALLIO Wäinö, 1887–1938; b. Finland, from Milford, NH 1932; Kondopoga; 91/4.

KANANEN (Kononen) Matti, 1906–1938; b. Oulunl., Kalajoki; from Canada 1931; Kem district, Sovporog, worker; 91/5.

KANGAS Kustaa, 1897–1937; b. Turunl., Kairila; from Canada 1931; Tunkua district, Andozero, logger; 91/6.

KANGAS Hilja, 1904(7?)–1938; b. Finland; 1931 from US; Interposyolok; 91/6.

KANGAS Matti, 1904–38; b. Finland, Keminl., Kylänkirkko, from US; Interposyolok, logger; 91/6.

KANGAS Urho, 1903–38; b. Finland, from US 1931; Kondopoga; 91/5.

KANGASNIEMI Hanna, 1906–38; b. Finland; from US 1932; Uhtua; 91/4.

KANGASNIEMI Antti (Hanna's father), 1878–1938; b. Finland; from US in 1932; Uhtua. There was a US-born son William—no info. 91/5.

KANKAANPÄÄ Kalle, 1889–38; b. Oulunl., Sievi; from Detroit 1933; Interposyolok, mechanic; 91/6.

KANKAANPÄÄ (Kangaspää) Sakari, 1880–1931; b. Oulunl.; from Canada; Petrozavodsk ski factory; 91/5.

KARHINEN Hanna, 1978–1938; b. Viipuri; from Seattle US in 1926; Petrozavodsk; 91/5.

KARI Artur, 1897–1938; b. Hämeenlinna, Piispala; from Canada 1932; Muyezersk district, Tumba, logger; 91/6.

KARI Kalle, 1910–1938; from Astoria, Oregon 1933; Padozero. logger; 91/6.

KARJALAINEN Kalle, 1912–1938, b. Finland; from US 1931; Latva, logger; 91/6.

KARJALAINEN Yegor (Heikki, Henry?), 1902–1938; b. Oulunl., Porssu; from Canada 1932; Uhtua district, Kannussuo, logger; 91/5.

KARLSSON Kaarlo, 1894–1938, b. Finland; from New York; Kondopoga; 91/5.

KAUPPI Leo, 1900–?, b. Finland and his wife

KAUPPI (Nyman) Hilda, 1896–1938, b. Finland, Pitkäranta, from New York 1931; Petrozavodsk; 91/5. Leo had a 10-year sentence.

KASARI (Kosuri) Antti, 1893–1938; b. Kuopionl.,Korvosalmi; from US 1931; Lososinnoye, logger; 91/6.

KEKKO Aarne (Ale), 1902–1952; b. Mikkelinl.; from US 1931; Petrozavodsk, Karelavto; 91/3.

KELA Johann, 1893–1938; b. Finland; from Canada 1932; Petrozavodsk ski factory; 91/5.

KEMPPAINEN Axel son of Kalle, 1907–1938; b. Finland, from Ladysmith, Canada 1931; Uhtua; 91/4.

KEMPPAINEN Valde, 1883–1938; b. Vaasanl.; from Canada 1931; Petrozavodsk, carpenter; 91/5. He and wife Maria had a 1915-Canadian born son Tauno. No info.

KERÄNEN Antti (Alarik), 1889–?; b. Finland; from US 1932; Petrozavodsk State farm; 91/5—a 3-year sentence.

KERTTULA Nestor, 1892–1938; b. Oulunl., Alavieska; from Eben Junction, Mich.1932; Uhtua, carpenter; 91/5.

KESANTO Martti, 1891–38; b. Finland, Kustaanp., Rymänkylä; from New York 1932; Aunus, Ilyinsk state farm ; 91/5.

KETOLA Eino, 1891–1938; b. F.Pyhäjoki, Säkylä; from US 1932; Petrozavodsk, carpenter; 91/5.

KETOLA Wäinö, 1892–1938; b. Porinl., Kiimajärvi; from Sudbury, Canada, 1931; Matrosa, logger; 91/6.

KIHLMAN Ville (Wilho), 1890–1938;b. Finland, Kaikkila; from Canada 1932; Padany. logger; 91/6.

KINNUNEN (Koivulehto) Otto, 1894–1946, b. Finland; From Ill., US 1932; Kondopoga; 91/3.

KIUKKOLA Johan, 1887–1938; b. Finland; from US in 1931; Petrozavodsk ski factory; 91/5.

KIVELÄ Fred, 1889–1938; b. F.Vaasanl., Lapua; from Canada 1933, had a higher education; Lososinnoye, mechanic; 91/6.

KIVISAARI Harold, 1906–1938, b. US, Kondopoga paper mill, worker; 91/5.

KIVISTÖ Karl, 1896–1938; b. F.Oulunl.,Uusikirkko; from US 1932; Kondopoga, construction worker; 91/5.

KOIVISTO Kustaa, 1883–1938; b. Finland; from South Porcupine, Canada 1931; Petrozavodsk ski factory; 91/5.

KOIVISTOINEN Rauni, 1914–1937; b. Finland; from Canada 1931; Padozero, tractor-driver; 91/6.

KOIVUKANGAS Juho, 1890–1938; b. F. Oulunl., Liminkä; from Canada 1931; Matrosa, logger; 91/6.

KOIVU (Koivula) Kalle, 1902–1937; b. Finland; from Canada 1932; Leningrad; 91/4.

KOIVU Onni, 1914–1938, b. US; Pryazha district, Kindasovo, tractor driver; 91/6.

KOIVULAAKSO Juho (John), 1898–1938; b. Finland; from Canada 1932; Kondopoga paper mill; 91/5.

KOIVULUOMA Jaakko, 1897–1938; b. Finland; from Temple, Maine US; Uhtua, Kannussuo, logger; 91/5.

KOIVUNIEMI Juho (John), 1899–1938; b. F. Oulunl., Jokikylä; from Canada 1932; Matrosa, tractor driver; 91/6.

KOKKO Matti, 1892–1938; b. F. Vaasanl.; from Canada 1931; Rukajärvi, saw-setter; 91/6.

KOMI Juho, 1890–1938; b. F. Lahti; from US 1931; Rugozero, logger; 91/6.

KORHONEN Johannes, 1890–?; b. Finland; from Canada; Petrozavodsk, state farm N 2; 91/6—a 3-year sentence.

KORPI Arvo, 1892–1937; b. Normarkinp., Harhala; from US 1931; Petrozavodsk construction; 91/5.

KORPI Jussi (Jaakko), 1893–1938; b. F. Vaasanl.; from Ishpeming Mich. 1932; Vilga, logger; 91/6.

KORPI Oskar, 1891–1938; b. Finland; from Quincy, Mass. 1932; Petrozavodsk Karelavto; 91/2.

KOSKELA Emil son of Juho, 1888–1938; b. Finland; (might be directly from Finland); Louhi district, Plotina; 91/5.

KOSKELAINEN Aleksander, 1889–1938; b. F.Impilahti; from US 1928; Karelavto, shop steward; (91/1).

KOSKI Hugo, 1908–1937; b. F. Vaasanl.; from Canada 1931; Tunkua district, Lehto; 91/6.

KOSKI Kalle, 1888–1938;; b. F. Mikkelinl., Pieksämäki; from US 1934; Prionezhye district, Polovina. logger; 91/6.

KOSKINEN Aarne, 1907–1938, b. US; from US with family 1923; Prionezhye district, Pyazhiyeva Selkä, mechanic; 91/3.

KOSKINEN Benjamin (Aarne's father). His trial is described in "R.E." Family has rehabilitation papers.

KOSKINEN Sylvia Herman's daughter, 1905–38. from Canada 1935; Kondopoga, seamstress; 91/5.

KOSKINEN Yrjö, 1897–1938; b. Helsinki; from New York 1931; Rugozero railway construction; 91/6.

KOTILA Tauno, 1914–1938; b. Finland; from Canada; Matrosa, logger; 91/6.

KUFFAL Matti 1889–? and brother

KUFFAL Wäinö 1891–?; both b. Finland, Oulunl., Kusmoniemi; from Van Hook N.Dakota 1931; Pryazha district logging camps, loggers; both in 91/6—10-year sentences.

KUULA Leo-Niilo, 1909–1938, b. Canada, Carson Mines; from Canada 1932; Petrozavodsk, musician; 91/5.

KUUSINIEMI Yrjö, 1904–1937; b. Finland; from Detroit Mich.1931;

Petrozavodsk National theater, actor; 92/6.

KUJALA Eino, 1904–1938; b. F. Vaasanl., Kiviniemi; from US 1933; Uhtua, Kannussuo, foreman; 91/5.

KUNTO (Kuntz) Juho, 1898–1938; b. F. Viipurinl., Kumola; from US 1931; Petrozavodsk state farm N2; 91/6.

KUUSELA (Kakkonen) Anton (Antti), 1893–1938; b. F. Viipurinl., Yakkima; from US 1932; Padozero, logger; 91/6.

KYTÄLÄ Torsten, 1902–1938; b. F. Hämeenl., Tammela; from Canada 1932; Petrozavodsk, worker in trade organization; 91/5.

LAAKSO Eino, 1901–?, b. Finland; from Canada 1932; Pudozh, car and tractor station; 91/7—a 10-year sentence.

LAAKSO Toivo, 1892–1938; b. Finland; from Chicago US 1932; Onega plant; 91/7.

LAAKSO Urho, 1884–38; b. Tampere; from US 1930; Petrozavodsk, musician; 91/7.

LAATIKAINEN Aate, 1888–1938, b. in Russia in Ingria; from Canada 1934; Petrozavodsk, musician; 91/7.

LAHTI Arvid, 1910–?; b. US; from US 1931; Kondopoga; 91/7.

LAHTI Johan (John, Juho), 1908–1938; b. US Cape Cod Mass.; Uhtua, tractor driver; 91/7.

LAHTI Kaarlo, 1885–1937; b. Finland; from US 1931; Aunus district, Rajakontu;91/7.

LAHTI Kalle, 1885–1937; b. Finland; from Cobalt, Canada 1930; Aunus district, agriculture; 91/7.

LAINE August, 1893–?; b. Kuopionl., Lapinvesi; from US 1931; Petrozavodsk quarry worker; 91/7—a 10-year sentence.

LAINE Harry-Benny,1915–1938, b. US Fort Fosset; from US 1931; Petrozavodsk ski factory; 91/3.

LAINE Toivo, 1894–1938; b. F. Hämeenl.; from Detroit, Mich,; work place not indicated; 91/2.

LAINE Viktor, 1893–1938, b. F. Hämeenl.; from Canada 1933; Onega plant; 91/7.

LAITILA Matti, 1899–1938; b. F. Vaasanl., Ikkalanjärvi; from US in 1932; Rugozero logging camp; 91/7.

LAITINEN Juho, 1889–1938; b. Finland; from US 1932; Kem, painter; 91/7.

LAKKILA Matti, 1883–?; b. Helsinginl., Järkijärvi; from US 1931; Vilga, logger; 91/7—5 years of exile.

LAMPINEN Paavo, 1905–1938; b. F. Vaasanl, Alavanp.; from US 1931; Lososinnoye, driver; 91/7.

LAMPINEN Viktor, 1878–1938; b. Finland; from Sault St.Marie, Canada 1922; Uhtua; 91/9.

LANKILA Jaakko, 1877–1938; b. F. Kalajoki; from Canada; Pryazha district, Korza; 91/7.

LAPINSALO Eetu (Edward), 1895–1944; b. F. Oulunl.; from Canada 1931; Uhtua, theater producer; 91/4.

LATVALA Julius, 1887–?; b. Finland; from Duluth. Minn.1934(?); Petrozavodsk construction worker; 91/7—8-year sentence.

LAUHANEN Otto, 1897–?; b. Finland; from Canada 1932; Canadian-1917- born son—no info; 91/7. Otto—deported from USSR.

LAUKKANEN Antti, 1891–1938; b. Finland; from Rock, Mich.1932; Uhtua; 91/7.

LAUKKARINEN Wilho, 1899–1938; F. Mikkelinl, Salmi; from Canada 1931; Vilga, logger; 91/7.

LAULUMAA Markus, 1881–1938; b. Finland; from US 1923; Kondopoga, carpenter; 91/7.

LEHONEN (Lehtonen) Viljo, 1904–1938; b. F. Vaasanl.; from Canada 1932; Ski factory mechanic; 91/7.

LEHTO Emil, 1886–1938; b. Finland; from Canada 1931; Kondopoga, carpenter; 91/7.

LEHTO (Hulkkanen) Lauri, 1880–1938; b. Finland; from Foster Rhode Isl. in 20's; Uhtua; 91/3; Lauri's sons:

LEHTO (Hulkkanen) Wäinö, 1904–38; b. F.Ruovesi; from US in 1932; Solomennoye power station; 91/3.

LEHTO (Hulkkanen) Urho, 1910–38; b. Finland; from US 1932; Kiestinki; 91/3.

LEINO Frank, 1884–1938; b. F. Vaasanl., Kirkonkylä; 1931 from Orr, Minn.US; Kondopoga, carpenter; 91/7.

LEINO Tuure-William, 1898–1938; b. Finland; from Maine, US 1931; Kondopoga district, Suna, carpenter; 91/7.

LEIVO Hugo, 1888–1938;b. F. Mikkelinl., Kirkko; from US 1931; Matrosa, road-builder; 91/7.

LEIVONEN Karl, 1886–1938; b. Finland; from US 1931; Kondopoga construction worker; 91/7.

LENTOMÄKI (Letonmäki) Karl, 1897–1937; b. Finland; 1931 from Ludlow, Vermont; Kondopoga construction worker; 91/7.

LEPPÄ Otto, 1906–?; b. Finland; from US 1932; Pudozh district; 91/7.—3 years of exile.

LEPPÄLÄ Heikki, 1883–1938; b. Finland; from US 1932; Kondopoga logging center; 91/7.

LEPPÄNEN Kalle, 1889–1938; b. F. Vaasanl., Saarenjärvi; from Cobalt, Canada 1928; Aunus agricultural laborer; 91/7.

LESKINEN Matti, 1897–?, b. Finland; from US 1932; State farm N 2; 91/7—3-year sentence.

LIND Eino (Einar), 1910–1938; b. Finland; from Canada 1932; Vilga tractor station; 91/7.

LINDHOLM Wäinö, 1886–1938; b. Finland, Rukajärvi; from US 1931; Prionezhye district, Shoksha quarry worker; 91/7.

LINDQUIST Aino, 1900–1938; b. Finland; from US 1932; Uhtua, typist; 91/7.

LIUKKO Einar, 1905–1938; b. F. Kirimäenp.; from Canada 1931; Kondopoga construction; 91/7.

LONG Nikolai (Niilo), 1895–1938; b. F. Rajarenki; from US 1932; Aunus, agriculture worker; no information on two US-born sons; 91/9.

LUMIO Toivo, 1886–1938; b. Finland; from US 1932; Petrozavodsk, painter; 91/7.

LUOMA Aleksander, 1888–1938; b. F. Vaasanl., Liedenpohja; from US 1932; Muyezersk district Ondozero logging center; 91/7.

LUOMA Juho, 1894–1938; b. F. Vaasanl. Ylä-Karjala; from Canada 1931; Uhtua, carpenter; 91/3.

LUOMA Lauri, 1896–1938; b. F. Vaasanl., Mikonp., Pirti; from Detroit, Mich. 1931; Petrozavodsk, watchman; 91/6.

MÄENPÄÄ Juho, 1899–1937; b. F. Vaasanl.; from Canada 1933; Belomorsk, carpenter; 91/8.

MÄENPÄÄ Wäinö, 1903–1937; b. F. Vaasanl. Ähtäri; from Canada 1932; Uhtua odd jobs; 91/8.

MÄKELÄ Iisak, 1901–1938; b. Finland; from Ironwood, Mich. 1931; Yushkozero logger; 91/8.

MÄKELÄ Timo (Tuomas), 1898–1937; b. Finland; from Brookline, NH 1931; Repola. logger; 91/4.

MÄKI Aarne, 1909–1938; b. F. Oulunl.; from US 1932; Pai tractor driver; 91/8.

MÄKI Albert, 1916–?; b. Columbia, Canada; from Canada 1932; Uhtua, assistant bookkeeper; 91/8—a 10-year sentence.

MÄKI Hannes, 1891–38; b. F. Tampere, from Canada; Kondopoga, Sandal brick factory; 91/9.

MÄKI Jaakko, 1878–1938; b. F. Vaasanl., Matinp.; from Sandstone, Minn. 1933; Vilga garage worker; 91/3.

MÄKI John (Juho), 1879–1938; from US 1932; Vilga tractor station; 91/8.

MÄKI Walter, 1907–1938; b. Minn. USA, from US 1931; Uhtua carpenter; 91/8.

MÄKINEN Kalle, 1900–1938; b. Finland; from Canada 1931; Matrosa logger; 91/8.

MALEN Akseli, 1891–1938; b. F. Turku-Porinl.; from US 1931; Kondopoga carpenter; No info on US-born sons Roy, 1913, and Paul, 1914; 91/8.

MANNER Harry, 1905–1938; b. F. Kerimäenp.; Petrozavodsk ski factory; 91/8.

MANNINEN Jalmari, 1885–?; b. Finland; from Cobalt, Canada 1931; Aunus, agriculture laborer; 91/9—a 5-year sentence.

MARTTILA Albert, 1908–1938; b. Cloquet, Minn.; Petrozavodsk, musician; 91/8.

MATTSON Eino, 1909–38; b. Helsinki; from US 1931; Kondopoga paper mill plumber; 91/8.

MATTSON Johan, 1884–1938; b. Finland, from US 1932; Uhtua logging center; 91/8.

MATTILA Kalle, 1881–1938; b. Finland; from US, State of Washington; Shoksha quarries; 91/8.

MATTSON Henry (Heikki), 1891–1938; b. F. Kotka; from Worcester, Mass. 1932, and his wife

MATTSON Lempi, 1894–39; b. Finland, Ylikylä; both arrested from Uhtua; 91/8. No info of American-born, 1920, daughter Aune.

MATTSON Taisto, 1915–1938; b. US; from US 1932; Kondopoga fire department; 91/8.

MAUNUMÄKI Matti, 1899–1938; b. F. Vaasanl., Lahtaja; from Canada. Kirkland Lake 1932 (?); Petrozavodsk state farm N 2; 91/8.

MERILÄ Alfred, 1903–38; b. Finland, Pulkkila; from Hancock, Mich. in 1931; Petrozavodsk, musician; 91/8.

MERILÄINEN Henry (Heikki), 1888–1938, b. Finland; from US 1930; Onega plant; 91/8.

METSOLA Jalo, 1906–38; b. Finland; from Detroit, Mich. 1931; Petrozavodsk ski factory; 91/8.

MIKKONEN Eino, 1905–38; b. F. Vaasanl. Kuoppalank.; from Cape Cod US 1931; Uhtua, saw-setter; 91/8.

MIKKONEN Juho son of Kustaa, 1903–1938; b. Finland; from Canada 1932; Uhtua logger; 91/8.

MIKKONEN Juho son of Victor, 1908–1938; b. Finland; from Canada in 1933; Uhtua logger; 91/8.

MILLER Axel, 1905–57; b. Sweden, from Cleveland, Ohio 1932; worked in Kirov region; 91/6.

MINKINEN Sulo, 1906–1938; b. US, arrived from Finland; Lososinnoye driver; 91/8.

MOILANEN Heikki, 1904–1938; b. Finland; from US 1931; Matrosa, logger; 91/8.

MOILANEN Henrik (Heikki), 1898–1938; b. F. Viipurinl.; from Canada 1931; Solomennoye power station; 91/8.

MOISIO Juho (Johan), 1877–1938; b. F. Vaasanl.; from US 1931; Kondopoga logger; 91/8.

MULTAMäKI Juho, 1880–1930; b. F. Vaasanl., Kirkonk.; from US 1932; Uhtua, Kannussuo, logger; 91/8.

MURTOMÄKI Aimo-Ilmari, 1901–1938; b. Finland; from Canada 1932; Kondopoga district, Matkachi sanatorium, worker; 91/8.

MURTONEN Matti, 1888–1938; b. F. Vaasanl. Sarvijoki; from US 1930; Matrosa, blacksmith; 91/8.

MYLLÄRI Otto, 1898–1938, b. Finland; from Fairport, Ohio 1932(?); Kondopoga district, Sandala; 91/8.

MYLLYKANGAS Tauno, 1909–1938; b. F. Vaasanl. Perkovo; from Canada 1931; Vilga, electrician; 91/8.

NAAMANKO Pekka, 1882–1938; b. F. Kuusamo; from Canada 1932; Uhtua Kannussuo logger; 91/9.

NÄRHI (Närki) Otto, 1879–1938; b. F. Kuopionl., Rautalampi; from US 1932; Petrozavodsk ski factory; 91/3.

NELSON Enoch, 1897–1938; b. US; from San Francisco 1921; Uhtua, industrial enterprise; 91/2.

NENONEN Pekka, 1905–1938; b. F. Viipurinl., Kärkijoki; from Canada 1931; Pai, logger; 91/9.

NEULANEN Nikolai, 1884–1938; b. F. Oulunl.; from Canada, 1930; Uhtua, Kannussuo, logger; 91/9.

NIEMI Eino, 1907–1938; b. F. Vaasanl., Kaihia; from US 1934; Lososinnoye garage worker; 91/9.

NIEMI John, 1873–1938; b. Finland; from US 1932; Aunus agriculture worker; 91/9.

NIEMI Nestor, 1901–1938; b. US; from US 1932; Kondopoga paper mill; 91/9.

NIEMI Einar, 1906–1938; b. ?; from Fairport, Ohio; Aunus, worker; 91/2.

NIIRANEN Frans (Frank), 1885–1938; b. F. Turunl., Sonnuilank.; from S.Dakota 1932; 91/9.

NIKANDER Svante, 1882–1938; b. F. Karila; from US 1931; Vilga worker; 91/9.

NURMI Arthur Viktor's son, 1900–1938; b. F. Turku; from New York, 1930; Petrozavodsk construction ; 91/2.

NURMI Oiva Viktor's son, 1901–1938; b. F .Turku; from New York 1931; Petrozavodsk, dentist; 91/2. He brought all the dental equipment from the US at his own expense.

NYKÄNEN Juho, 1876–1937; b. F. Kuopionl. Rautalampi; from Canada 1932; Interposyolok blacksmith; 91/9.

OJA Aleksi (Elias), 1892–1938; b. Finland; from US 1931; Kondopoga, Lenlesstroi; 91/9.

OJA (Ojalehto) Armas, 1887–1938; b. Finland; from Baltimore, US 1931; Kondopoga; 91/4.

OJA Lempi, Aleksi's wife, from personal NKVDA file 4641—also arrested.

OKSA Wäinö Matti's son, 1882–1938; b. Finland, from US 21.04.32; Kondopoga farm worker; 91/9.

OKSA Jussi Matti's son, 1887–37; from NKVDA file 145: executed in 1937. All other data same—brothers.

OKSANEN Juho (Ely), 1897–1938; b. Finland; from Canada 1932; Petrozavodsk; 91/9.

PÄÄKKÖNEN Matti, 1898–1938; b. Finland; from Chicago Ill.1930; Petrozavodsk worker; 91/10.

PAASI (Paasio) Jalmar, 1898–?; b. Finland; from New York 1931; Petrozavodsk musician; 91/10/

PAASO Hugo, 1892–1938; b. Finland; from Waukegan, Ill. 1931; Petrozavodsk college; 91/2.

PAAVOLA Matti, 1902–1938; b. Finland; from Canada 1931; Petrozavodsk state farm N 2; 91/10.

PAJALA (Pahkala) Heikki 1909–?; b. ?; from Kelso, Wash. 1933; State farm N 2; 91/10—a 3-year sent.

PAJU Emil, 1878–1938; b. F. Vaasanl.; from US 1931; Kiestinki, mason; 91/10.

PAJUNEN (Paju) Jalmar, 1895–1944; b. Finland; from Peabody, Mass. 1931; Kondopoga construction; 91/4.

PASSI Einari, 1898–1938; b. Finland; from Canada; Vilga logger; 91/10.

PASSILA (Pasila) Anton,1880–?; b. F. Vyborg prov.; from US 1931; 91/10—5-year sent.

PEHKONEN Lasse, 1893–1938; b. Finland; from Canada 1931; Onega plant worker; 91/10.

PEKOLA Matti, 1899–1938; b. F. Oulunl., Nivalanp.; from Canada 1931; Muyezersk district, Ondozero, tractor driver; 91/10.

PELKONEN Tauno, 1906–1938; b. F. Kuopionl., Ristonp.; from Canada; 91/10.

PELTONEN Kaarlo (Kalle), 1886–1938, b. Finland; from Canada 1932; Kondopoga paper mill, blacksmith; 91/10.

PELTONEN Matti, 1896–1938; b. Finland; from Astoria, Oregon 1931; Kondopoga fire department, driver; 91/10.

PESONEN Armas, 1905–?; b. Helsinki; from New York 1932; Petrozavodsk Radio Committee; 91/10—a 5-year sentence.

PETTERSON Oskar, 1886–1938; b. F.Mikkeli; from Oregon US in 1923; Kondopoga, logging; 91/10.

PIETILÄ Alfred, 1911–1938. b. US; Petrozavodsk, driver; 91/10.

PIETILÄ Wäinö, 1892–?; b. Finland; from US 1932; Lososinnoye garage; 91/10—a 10-

year sentence.

PIIPARINEN (Piipari) Juho,1885–1938; b. F., Viipurinl., Parikkala; from US 1931; Kondopoga construction; 91/10.

PIISPANEN Eino, 1903–1938; b. Finland; from Cobalt, Canada 1931; Padozero logger; 91/10.

PUUSTEL Emil, 1888–1938; b. F. Kotka; from Canada 1932; Kem worker; 92/5.

PYYKKÖ Mikko, 1884–1938; b. Finland; from Berkley, Cal. 1931; Pryazha district, Kindasovo; 91/10.

RAJAKANGAS Helmi (Hilma), 1906–1938; b. Finland; from Canada 1932; Kondopoga; 91/11.

RANTA Emil, 1888–1938; b. F. Viipuri; from Canada 1931; Vilga logger; 91/11.

RANTA Oskari, 1886–1938. b. F. Turku; in 1931 from US; Uhtua, communal services department; 91/11.

RANTALA Toivo, 1883–1938; b. Finland; from Astoria, Oregon 1932; Onega plant; 91/2.

RAUTIAINEN Janne-Jalmari (Jack), 1885–1938, b. Finland; from Toronto, Canada; Petrozavodsk; construction; 91/11.

REINO Frans, 1905–1938; b. US (?); from US 1932; Kondopoga; 91/11.

RINNE Karl, 1894–1938, b. Finland; from New York 1932; Petrozavodsk; 92/6.

RINTALA Aleksi, 1904–1938; b. F. Vaasanl. Teuvanp.; from Canada 1931; Matrosa, logger; 91/11.

ROSSI Viktor, 1889–1938; b. F. Vaasanl. Urapainen; from Canada(?); Uhtua, carpenter

RUOTSI Pekka, 1882–1938; b. F. Kuopionl.; from US 1931; Kondopoga Sunastroi; 91/11.

RUUSKANEN Uuno, 1908–38; b. F. Oulunl. Kemink.; from Cherry, Minn.;Pryazha road-building; 91/11.

SAARI Elias (Ely), 1898–1938, b. Finland; from Port Chester, US 1932; Kondopoga paper mill; 91/12.

SAARI John (Juho), 1900–1938; b. Chassel, Mich.(?); from US 1932; Petrozavodsk, "Exportles"; 91/12.

SAARI Toivo Alexander's son, 1892–1937; b. Finland; from Canada 1933; Kondopoga; 91/1.

SAARI Toivo Alexander's son, 1910–1938; b. Canada; Uhtua. logger; 91/12.

SAARI Kalle, 1888–38; b. F. Hämeenl, Virola; from Mass. US in 1931; Karelavto; 91/12.

SAASTAMOINEN Robert, 1888–1937, b. Finland, from Ishpeming, Mich. 1933; Uhtua; 91/2.

SAKSA Toivo, 1904–1938; b. F. Hämeenl., Itäjärvi, from Canada 1931 and brother

SAKSA Eino, 1893–1938; same data; both worked in Matrosa; 91/12.

SALMI Kalle, 1897–1938; b. F. Turunl,. Kankaanpää; from Chicago, Ill. 1931; Padany, worker; 91/12.

SALMINEN Aarne, 1903–1938; b. Finland; from US 1931; Kondopoga, painter; 91/12.

SALMINEN Juho, 1890–1938, b. Finland; from Canada 1931; Kondopoga Lenstroi, worker; 91/12.

SALO Erland, 1896–?; b. F. Vyborg prov., from US 1931; Petrozavodsk, mason; 91/12—a 10-year sent.

SALO Gustav, 1884–1938; b. Finland; from Balsam, Minn. 1931; Kondopoga paper mill; 91/12.

SALO Henry, 1889–?; b. Vaasanl. Lapua; from Cleveland, Ohio, 1931 and his wife

SALO Emilia, 1892–?; b. F.; all other data the same; 91/12—both got 5-year sentences, nothing known about their future fate and that of their infant son.

SALO Toivo, 1917–1938; b. S. Porcupine, Canada; from Newberry, Mich.1931; Petrozavodsk Music school student; 91/12.

SALO Violette, 1914–1938, b. US; from US; Petrozavodsk, homemaker; 91/12.

SALO Yrjö, 1898–1938; b. Finland; from Canada 1932; Vilga logger; 91/12.

SALOMAA Nestor, 1880–1938; b. F. Mikkelinl., Mäntyharjanp.; from Canada 1932; Kondopoga, carpenter; 91/12.

SÄNTTI Jalmar Nestor's son, 1895–1938; b. F. Vaasanl.; from Canada 1931; Ski factory; 91/1.

SÄNTTI Urho Nestor's son, 1891–1938; b. F. Vaasanl.; from US 1932; Petrozavodsk; 91/12.

SAUKKO Henrick, 1905–1938; b. Finland; from Canada 1931; Kondopoga Sunastroi; 91/12.

SAVINIEMI Eelis Teodor, 1898–1938, from US; Uhtua, agriculture worker; 91/12.

SEVANDER Kalle, 1895–1943; b. F. Oulu; from Vancouver, Canada 1931; Petrozavodsk, Karelles; 91/3.

SIIKANEN Kalle, 1893–1938; b. Finland, from Cobalt Canada 1926; Aunus agriculture workers; 91/9. His wife:

SIIKANEN Lempi was arrested at the same time but she doesn't figure in any papers.

SIMANSON Sylvia, 1907; Kondopoga paper mill; 91/12. Deported from the country. No info on whether her husband and two children joined her somewhere.

SIMILÄ Jaakko, 1889–1938; b. F. Oulunl.; from Canada 1932; Uhtua carpenter; 91/12.

SIPPOLA (Siippola) Juho, 1889–1938; b. F. Porinl, Annilak.; from US 1932; Kiestinki. painter; 91/12.

SIVULA Johannes (Jussi), 1883–1938, b. F. Vaasanl. Laupijärvi; from Canada in 1934; Muyezersk district, blacksmith; 91/12.

SMOLANDER Erkki, 1885–1938; b. F. Korsemäki, Varnasjärvi, from Canada 1933; Interposyolok, logger; 91/12.

SOLKELA Severi (Seth), 1902–1938; b. US; from Chassel, Mich.1932; Kiestinki House of culture; 91/12.

SOMARI Eero, 1904–1938; b. F. Vaasanl., Kauppila; from Canada 1934; Segozero district, Padany logger; 91/12.

STENFORS Erkki, 1909–1938; b. F. Turku-Porinl.; from Canada 1931; Petrozavodsk, Repair shops; 92/1.

STORM Herman 1886–?; b. F. Vaasanl., Heikkilä; from US 1932; Kiestinki district, logger; 91/12—a 10-year sent.

TABEL Eino, 1904–1937; b. Finland; from US 1932; Louhi; 92/1 and his wife:

TABEL Lilja, 1909–1938; b. F. Visajärvenp.same data; Louhi district quarry workers; 92/1.

TAKALA Iisakki, 1883–1938; b. F. Vaasanl., Peräseinäjoenp.; from Ironwood, Mich. 1931; Petrozavodsk sawmill; 92/1.

TAKALA Jalmari, 1893–1938; b. F. Sakarinp.; from US 1932; Kondopoga paper mill; 92/1.

TALONEN William (Ely), 1899–1938; b. Finland; from Canada 1931;Pai logger; 92/1.

TAMMINEN Toivo, 1887–1938; b. F. Kuorvesi, Pihlaisto; from Canada 1931; Kondopoga, constructor; 92/1.

TANNER Mauno, 1887–1938; b. F. Viipurinl., Pohjanjärvenp.; from US 1932; Uhtua; 92/1.

TELIN Kustaa, 1886–1938; b. F. Hämeenl. Janakkolampi; from US 1931; Kondopoga paper mill.

TENHO Einari, 1889–1938; b. F. Kulmo; from US 1932; Petrozavodsk, construction; 92/1.

TENHUNEN Matti, 1887–1937; b. F. Kuopionl., Kiuruvesi; from US 1931; Petrozavodsk; 91/3.

TENHUNEN Nestor, 1884–1938; b. F. Vaasanl., Niinilehti; from US 1922 to Kuzbass; Kondopoga district, Uusikylä, logger; 92/1.

TERHONEN Johan, 1903–1938; b. Finland; from US 1932; Lososinnoye, garage; 92/1.

TIITINEN Jaakko, 1903–1937; b. Finland; from US 1932; Kondopoga; 92/6.

TOLMANEN Juho, 1888–1938; b. Finland; from Canada 1932; Petrozavodsk; Onega plant; 92/1.

TOLONEN David, 1880–1940; b. F. Kuopionl.; from Webster's Corner, Canada 1932; Vilga logger; 91/1.

TOLONEN Eino,1888–1938; b. F. Oulunl, Jyrönsalmi; from Detroit, Mich. 1931; Kondopoga mason; 92/1.

TORNIAINEN Valde, 1904–1938; b. Helsinki; from Canada. 1931; Lindozero logger; 92/1.

TOUKO Aarne, 1910–1944; b. Finland; from Ohio, US 1932; Petrozavodsk; 91/6.

TUKIAINEN Hannes, 1907–?; b. Finland; from Canada 1932; Petrozavodsk laborer; 92/1—a 3-year sent.

TUOMAINEN Axel, 1895–1937; b. Finland; from US 1932; Kondopoga Lenlesstroi; 92/1 and his wife

TUOMAINEN Lempi, 1897–?; b. Finland; same data; 92/1—a 5-year sentence.

TUOMINEN Wäinö, 1904–1938; b. F. Oulu; from Detroit, Mich. 1931; Syamozero tractor-driver; 92/1 and his wife:

TUOMINEN Lydia 1898–1938; b. Finland; same data; Syamozero seamstress; 92/1.

TUOMINEN George (Yrjö), 1896–1888; b. Finland; from US 1932; Prionezhye district, Velikaya Guba; 92/6.

TUOMISTO Jalmar, 1898–1938; b. Finland; from Canada 1931; Kondopoga paper mill; 92/1.

TUURI Jenny, 1884–1938; b. US; from US 1932 (on basis of Aronen's file); Uhtua children's home; 92/1. Her husband:

TUURI Leonid, 1881–1938; b. Finland; from US 1932 (on basis of NKVDAlbum N 8). No info on their son Tuuri Leonid, b.1908, US.

TUUTIJÄRVI Antti, 1897–1928, b. F. Oulunl; from Canada 1931; Uhtua; 91/2, 92/1. His wife:

TUUTIJÄRVI Hilja, 1903–1938, b. Finland; from Canada 1931; Uhtua; 92/1.

UITTI Toivo, 1903–1937; b. F. Vaasanl.; from Canada 1931; Lososinnoye garage; 92/6.

ULLAKKO Toivo, 1915–1938; b. US Embarrass, Minn.; from US 1931; Petrozavodsk, mechanic; 92/4.

UNKURI John, 1891–1938; b. F. Vaasanl. Yläjärvi; from US 1930; Uhtua; 92/4.

USENIUS Arthur, 1888–1937; b. Finland; from US 1922 (?); Uhtua; 91/9.

VÄÄNÄNEN Kaarlo, 1905–1938; b. F. Kuopionl. Keitali; from US 1932; Kondopoga, Sandal; 92/3.

VALENIUS Sulo, 1908–1938; b. Finland; from US (?); Latva logger; 92/2.

VÄLIMÄKI TOIVO, 1911–?; b. ?; from Baltimore US 1933; Nyrki tractor base; 92/2.

VAINIO Emil, 1894–1938; b. Finland; from US (?); Kondopoga, Sandal; 92/3.

VAINIO Eino, 1912–?; b. Finland; from US 1932; Petrozavodsk; 92/2 3 years of exile; and his brother:

VAINIO Onni, 1904–?, all other data the same;

VAINIO Voitto, 1913–1937; b. US (?); from US in 1932; Kondopoga; 92/6.

VARONEN Hanna, 1893–1938; b. F. Syysmäki; from US 1933; Belomorsk, sawmill; 92/2.

VARONEN Emil, 1909–1938; b. Finland; from US 1933; Belomorsk sawmill; 92/2.

WEST Emil, 1897–1938; b. F. Vaasanl. Jurva; from Canada 1932; Kondopoga logging camp; 92/3. His wife:

WEST Mary (Maya), 1907–1938; b. F. Vaasanl. Lapua; Kondopoga paper mill cleaner; 92/3.

VIGER Gabriel, 1885–1938; b. F. Vaasanl.Alasjärvi; from Detroit, Mich. 1932; Vilga blacksmith; 92/2.

VIIK Akseli, 1910–?; b. Finland; from US 1932; Solomennoye; 92/2.

VIITANEN Aate (Atle), 1884–1938; b. Finland; from US 1932; Petrozavodsk ski factory; 92/2.

VIITANEN Yrjö, 1899–1938; b. Finland; from US 1932; Kondopoga, Sandal; 92/3.

VILEN Karl, 1880–1938; b. Finland; from New Jersey US 1932; Uhtua; 92/1.

VILENIUS Yrjö, 1903–?; from US 1932; Petrozavodsk driver; 92/2—a 5-year sentence.

VILJAKAINEN Toivo, 1904–1938; b. F. Mikkelinl.; from Canada 1932; Uhtua Kannussuo; 92/2.

VILJAMAA Niilo, 1889–1938; b. Oulunl. Kalamaa; from Iron River, Minn.; Pai logger; 92/2.

VILJASALO (Vainio) Onni, 1904–?; b. Finland; from Canada 1932; Petrozavodsk power plant; 92/2. 3 years of exile.

VILMAN (Vahlman) Frans, 1873–1938; b. F. Kajani; 1923—Kuzbass, returned on visa 1932; Olonets district, Vidlitsa; 92/2. His son:

VALLIN Emil son of Frans, 1909–1938, b. US New York; from US 1932; Olonets district, Vidlitsa mechanic; 92/2.

VIRKKANEN Otto, 1905–1938; b. F. Oulunl; from Canada 1932; Matrosa logger; 92/2.

VIRTA Seth, 1883–1938; b. Finland; from "America" 1922; Olonets district, Ilyinsk grain storage; 92/2.

VIRTANEN Helena, 1900–1938; b. Finland; from US 1932; Petrozavodsk, Ski factory; 92/2.

VIRTANEN Heikki, 1893–1938; b. Finland, from US 1932; Petrozavodsk ski factory; not in "Carelia," protocol n 27, evidently husband of Helena.

VIRTANEN Lauri, 1898–1938; b. Finland; from US 1932; Uhtua; 91/3.

VIRTANEN Martti, 1904–1938; b. Finland; from US 1932; Kondopoga Lenstroi; 92/3.

VIRTANEN Viljo, 1899–38; b. Finland; from Canada 1932; Kondopoga paper mill; 92/3.

VONKAVAARA Hannes, 1912–1938; b. US, from US 1932; Uhtua Kis-Kis lumber camp; 92/2.

VUORI Juho Kustaa's son, 1894–1938; b. Vaasanl.; from US 1932; Olonets district, Ilyinsk state farm; 92/2.

VUORI Juho Konsta's son,1891–1938; b. Uudenmaanl.; from Granitville, Vermont 1932; Kondopoga paper mill; 92/1.

YLINEN Matti; b.1887, Porinl. Tarka; from Canada 1933; Lososinnoye logger; 92/5—no sentence indicated.

YLITALO Johan-Gustav, 1881–1938; b. Finland; from Canada; Uhtua; 92/5; his son:

YLITALO Helge, 1915–1938; b. Finland; from Canada; Uhtua; 92/5.

The TOTAL rehabilitated in "Carelia":

Arrested and rehabilitated—410. Among them:

men	79
women	31
arrivals from the USA	270
arrivals from Canada	40

APPENDIX 2.

Victims of Stalinism rehabilitated in the newspaper "PETROZAVODSK" in 1994 (date indicated)

ALANEN Erkki, 1900–1938; b. Finland; from US 1932; Karelavto; 11.03.

BIRCH Emil; b. F. Turunl., Uusikirkko; from Canada 1931; electrician; 22.04.

FINBERG Wäinö, 1887(?)–1938; b. F. Turunl., Kolpio; from Superior, Wisc. 1931; Publishing house, editor; 25.03.

GRANDEL Toivo; b. Finland, 1898; from Detroit, Mich. 1933; Karelavto; 11.03.

HANNULA Andrew; b. 1913, New York; from US 1932; electrician; 22.04.

HAUTALA Theodor; b. 1910 (?) New York; from New York 1931; radio station, purschased radio equipment in US and brought it along; 22.04.

HELLBERG Martha; from US 1932; Petrozavodsk; 13.05. Arrived with HELLBERG Otto of whom no info.

HOFFREN Einar; b. F. Kuopionl., Euranp. 1896; from US 1931; barber, worked at theater; 25.03.

JOKELA Juho; b.1883, Hämeenlinna; from US 1931; carpenter at school; 22.04.

KANTAKOSKI August, 1905–1938; b. F. Vaasanl., from Canada 1932; Petrozavodsk ski factory; 11,03.

KARHU Lauri; b. US 1902; from Newark US; electrician; 22.04.

KLEMOLA Eeva; b. 1881, F. Kuopionl.; from Detroit, USA 1932; ("R.E." p.p. 120–121); retired; 29.04. Her husband:

KLEMOLA Edward who did not return after his arrest, no info.

KOIVU Kaarlo, arrived with wife Elvira and son Raymond from LA, Cal 1934; no other factual data; 29.04.

KORTES (Lähdeskorpi) Victor; b. 1992, F. Turunl., Toinijoki; from Mich. US 1931; driver; 25.03.

KUUSISTO Paavo, 1902–1938; b. F. Porinl. Ruosniemi; 1931 from Canada; Petrozavodsk ski factory; 11.03.

LAAKSO Eero; b. F. Turunl., Sarvenhäminä; from New York 1931; radio technician; 22.04.

LAAKSO Uuno; Petrozavodsk office worker; 22.04.

LAINE Evert; Petrozavodsk ski factory; 22.04.

NIEMI Antti, 1886; b. Vaasanl., Alajärvi; from Brooklyn, NY 1931; Petrozavodsk carpenter; 22.04.

NIEMINEN Karl, 1885–1938; b. F. Porkkalanl., Danola; from US 1932; Petrozavodsk ski factory.

NYLANDER Heino; b. Viipuri, 1908; from Minneapolis, Minn. 1931; Karelavto; 11.03.

OKSANEN Anna; b. Finland, 1898; from Detroit, Mich.1932; retiree; 22.04.

PARRAS Emil, from Astoria, Oregon, 1932; well-known Finnish writer; Petrozavodsk; 22.04.

PUTKONEN Jalmar-Juho, 1891–1938; b. F. Viipurinl., Parikkala; from Canada 1932; Petrozavodsk ski factory; 11.03.

RANTANEN Toivo, 1904–1938; b. Finland; from Detroit, Mich. 1922; professor at Teachers' college Petrozavodsk; 8.04 and his wife:

RANTANEN Tyyne, 1883–1955(?); b. Helsinki; same data; ("R.E." p.p. 64–65).

RAUTANEN Lauri, 1887–?; b. F. Suoniemenp.; from Ontagonon, Mich, 1932 ("R.E," p.p.94-95); 15.04.

RIIHONEN Harold (Heikki); b. 1922, United States; worker in Petrozavodsk; 22.04.(date may refer to arrival in Russia).

SAUSO Theodor, 1890–1938; b. Finland, Vaasanl.Tuomaksenp., Vähäkylä; from US 1932; Petrozavopdsk printer; 25.03.

TERHO Ida (1887/1897?/–1938); b. Finland; from US 1932; Petrozavodsk state farm N 2;18.03

WIRTANEN Eino, 1902–1938; b. F. Turku-Porinl., Kokomäki; from Canada 1931 and 1932; Petrozavodsk electrician; 22.04.

The TOTAL considering those rehabilitated in "Petrozavodsk":
32 victims. Among them:

men	28
women	4
arrivals from the USA	25
arrivals from Canada	5
country of departure unknown	2

APPENDIX 3.

Victims of Stalinism not found in rehabilitation lists but registered in albums (A) and/or protocols (P)
** indicates—to be found only in Protocol.*
*** indicates—family has rehabilitation, or the information comes from files).*

AALTO Leo, 1912–?, b. F. Rauma; from Canada 1931; Tunkua, logger; A-28.

AHOKAS Elis, 1883–1938, b. Finland, from Cobalt, Canada in 1926; "Säde" Aunus; A-5.**

ALALANKOSKI Vilho, 1905–?; b. F. Turku-Porinl., Kehniö; from Canada; Uhtua, worker; A-23.

ALHO Karl, 1895–?; b. F. Turku-Porinl., Karkuu; from Canada, 1831; Petrozavodsk, furniture factory; A-32.

ARONEN Kalle, 1894–1938, b. Finland, Tampere; from US 1931; Petrozavodsk, driver; P-1.**

AUTIO Oskari, 1887–?, b. Vaasanl, Jokikylä; from US 1933; Uhtua; A-25.

BELMAN Karl, 1887–?; b. F. Tornio; from Canada 1922; Uhtua, mechanic; A-2.

BJÖRBACKA Aleksander, 1904–?; b. F. Evijärvenp., Jokikylä; from US 1931; Ondozero, logger; A-26;

BJÖRN Eino, 1911–?; b. US, Angora, Minn.; from US 1932; Vilga, mechanic; A-10.

DAHLBERG Olavi, 1914–1938; b. US State of Washington; from US 1931; Petrozavodsk, musician; P-2. His mother:**

DAHLBERG Mary, 1892–?; b. Finland; was in prison for 5 years; was released and departed for Finland, where she passed away. She isn't registered in any books.**

DAHLBOM Vilho, 1899–1938; b. F. Turju-Porinl., Pori; from Canada 1931; Uhtua, driver; P-10.*

EEROLA Urho, 1892–?; b. F. Vaasanl.; from Canada 1931; Petrozavodsk construction; A-17.

EKLUND Frans-Konrad, 1891–?; b. F. Uudenmaanl., Nurmijärvenp.; from US 1931; Petrozavodsk, Karelavto; A-38.

ELO Juho, 1889–?; b. F. Turunl., Haapakoski; from US 1931; Kondopoga, blacksmith; A-7.

ENQUIST Erkki, 1900–?; b. F. Tampere; from Canada 1931; Petrozavodsk; A-38.

ERICKSON (Palo) Karl, 1899–?; b. F. Oulu; from Detroit, US 1931; Kondopoga, Lennstroi; A-36.

ERKKILÄ Eino, 1908–?; b. Finland; from US 1932; Matrosa; A-16. His wife:**

ERKKILÄ Saimi 1904–94; from US 1932; returned from a gulag after over 20 years; P-3.**

ESKOLA Toivo, 1908–1938;b. F. Oulunl., Kirkonk.; from US 1931; Petrozavodsk, musician; P-4**

ESKOLIN August, 1894–?; b. F. Tampere; from Brooklyn, NY 1931; Kondopoga, mechanic; A-18.

FINNILÄ William, 1908–1938; b. US; from US 1936; garage mechanic; P-4 (was organizing a mass border crossing).

FORS Aili, 1895–1938; b. F. Oulunl., Kalajoki; from US in late twenties; Uhtua, rehab. in 92/3.

FORS Antti, 1878–1938, b. F. Oulunl, Kalajoki; from US in late 20's; Uhtua; P-1.

FORSMAN Kaarlo, 1900–?; b. F. Turun ja Porinl., Eurajoki; from Canada 1931;

Interposyolok logger; File-1073.

FORSMAN Nestor, 1876–?; b. F. Turku-Porinl.; from US 1932; Petrozavodsk, state farm N2; A-29.

FRILUND Keijo, 1908–1938; b. Chicago, US; from US 1931; Petrozavodsk ski factory; P-2.**

GILBERG Eino, 1899–?; b. Finland, Kuopionl., Iisalmi; from Canada 1932; Uhtu Pilsamo, logger; A-18.

GOLBERG John (Jussi), 1891–? ; b. F. Oulunl.; from US 1931; Uhtua. logger; P-A-163. (Olavi Golberg—his son, see app.1)

GRÖNHOLM Wäinö, 1901–?; b. F. Turku; from Canada 1931; Matrosa, logger; A-15.

HAKALA Iisakki, 1898–?; b. F. Vaasanl. Kurikka; from Cromwell. Minn. 1931; Kondopoga construction; A-36.

HAKALA William (Ben), 1910–?; b. Finland; from US 1931; Kondopoga logging center; A-35.

HAKALA Einari, 1912–?; b. ?; from Canada 1931; Matrosa logger; A-17.

HAKALA William, 1898–1938; b. Finland; from US 1930; Kondopoga, logger; P-17.

HAKANEN Karl,1887–1938; b. Finland, Juosilahti; from Quincy, Mass. 1932; Shoksha quarries; A-24.** His wife:

HAKANEN Judith, 1892–1953(?), returned after 10 years in a gulag; A-19.**

HALLIKAINEN Henrik, 1903–1938; b. F. Viipurinl.; from Canada 1933; Kondopoga logger; P-9.

HÄMÄLÄINEN Hieska, b.1881–?; b. Viipurinl., Hiitalanp.; from Canada 1932; Petrozavodsk ski factory; A-37.

HANKA (Honka?) Eero, 1908–?; b. F. Vaasanl., Tuomaksenp.; from Canada 1932; Tumba logger; A-24.

HÄNNINEN Antti, 1908–1938; b. F. Viipurinl.; from Canada (?); Padozero logger; P-13*

HANNULA Nikolai, 1902–?; b. F. Paavola, Alajärvi; from US 1931; Soroka (Belomorsk) sawmill; A-8.

HARJU Theodor, 1887–?; b. F. Turku; from US 1933; Uhtua, Kannussuo; A-12.

HARJU Tuomas 1910–1938; b. F. Vaasanl.; from Canada 1931; P-3.*

HEIKKILÄ Kusti (August), 1882–?; b. F. Vaasanl., Heikkilänkl.; from Gardner, Mass. 1933; Petrozavodsk ski factory; A-37.

HEIKKINEN Kalle, 1883–1938; b. Finland; from Canada 1932; Uhtua Kannussuo; A-19.

HEIKKINEN Wäinö, 1908–?; b. F. Kuopionl., Kirkko; from US 1931; Vilga (?) logger; A-7.

HEINILUOMA Nikolai,, 1898–?; b. Finland; from Canada 1931; Petrozavodsk ski factory, P-16.* His son:

HEINILUOMA Pentti, 1919–?; b. Canada; from Canada 1931; Petrozavodsk ski factory; A-34.

HEINO Karl Nestor's son, 1915–?; b. Finland, from Conneticut, US 1931; Kondopoga paper mill; A-36.

HEINO Kalle David's son, 1881–1938; b. Finland, from US 1932; Kontupohja construction; P-16.

HELANDER August, 1898–?; b. Finland; from Canada 1932; Kondopoga Sunastroi; A-38.

HELIN Evert, 1888–?; b. F. Vaasanl., Pohjanlahtimäki; from US 1932; File 4639.

HIETA Veikko, 1914–1938; b. US; from US 1931; Petrozavodsk Ski factory; P-2.** His brother:

HIETA Reino, 1914–1938; b. US, from US 1931; Petrozavodsk ski factory; P-17.**

HIETALA Oskari, 1890–1938; b. F. Vaasanl.; from Canada 1931; Petrozavodsk ski factory;P-3.**

HIIRONEN Albert, 1914–?; b. Detroit, US; from US 1931; P-16: sentence commuted for 5 years—attempt to cross border. In A-36 we read the following, "Both of his parents have been arrested".

HILTUNEN Jaakko, 1881–?; b. Finland; from US 1922 to Knösäs (fishing commune); A-6.

HOKKANEN Juho, 1887–1938; b. Kuopionl. Hankamäki; from US 1932; construction worker, Kiestinki; P-11

HILTUNEN Pekka,1884–1938; b. F. Kuopionl., Alapitkänp.; from Ontario, Canada 1931; Petrozavodsk ski factory welder; P-3.**

HOLOPAINEN Aaro, 1892–1938; b. F. Kuopionl., Ristovesi; from Mason, Wisc. 1932; Petrozavodsk state farm N 2 (see "R.E." p. 74); P-13.** His son:

HOLOPAINEN Toivo, 1915–1938; b. US, same data; P-16.**

HUHTALA France, 1904–?; b. F. Alavieksa; from Alberta, Canada 1931; Uhtua, carpenter; A-11.

HYVÄNEN Jukka (Juho), 1903–?; b. Finland; from Canada 1932; Interposyolok; A-33.

HYTÄNEN Iivari, 1900–?; b. F. Vaasanl., Liimatala; from Canada 1931; Matrosa, blacksmith; A-15.

HYVÄNEN Lauri, 1891–?; b. Finland, Oulu; from Canada 1930; A-15.

INGMAN Jalmar (Juho), 1886–1938; b. Finland; from Norwood, Mass. 1931; Kondopoga paper mill; P-3.**

ISAAKSON Tuomas, 1894–1938; b. USA; from USA 1931; Matrosa mechanic; A-16.**

ITKONEN Otto, 1901–?; b. F. Vaasanl.; from Canada 1931; Tumba logger. A-24.

JANHUNEN Paul, 1918–1938; b. Aberdeen, Wash., from US 1931; Petrozavodsk, Onega plant; P-3.**

JÄRVI Juho, 1891–?; b. Finland; from Canada; Petrozavodsk state farm N 2; A-22.

JÄRVI Matti, 1884–1938; b. F. Vaasanl., Alakylä; from Palmer, Mich. 1932; Vilga, logger; A-13.**

JOKI Johan, 1897–(death sent. was commuted for 10 years, no other info); b. F. Kemi; from US 1932; P-2.

JOKINEN Juho, 1887–?; b. F. Uudenmaanl., Helsinginp.; from Canada 1932; Kondopoga Sunastroi; A-38.

JOKINEN Kalle, 1895–?; b. F. Hämeenl., Kirken; from Canada 1930; Matrosa, logger; A-13.

JOKINEN Osmo, 1904–?; b. F. Turku-Porinl.; from Canada 1932; Uhtua, communication services; A-16

JOKINEN Toini, 1926–?; b. US; from US 1931; Petrozavodsk ski factory; A-34.

JUOPERI Matti, 1904–?; b. Finland; from Canada 1932; Matrosa logger; A-13.

JUVONEN Juho-William, 1900–?; b. F. Tampere; from Canada 1932; Onega plant; A-37.

JYLHÄ Antti, 1903–1938; b. Oulunl. Ylävieska; (probably from Finland. Relatives of a Jylhä-family that returned to US); Padozero logger; P-5. and his brother

JYLHÄ Esa, 1905–1938; P-26, all other info the same.

JYRKINEN Johan (John), 1883–?; b. F. Viipurinl.; from US 1933; Kondopoga paper mill; A-33.

KAARTINEN Matti 1907–?; b. US, from Waukegan Ill., 1931; Syamozero tractor driver; A-2.

KALLIO Lauri, 1896–?; b. Finland, Forsa; from Washburn, Wisc. US 1932; Belomor district Ondozero; A-38.

KALLIO Markus, 1898–?; b. Finland; from US 1932; returned after a 25-year prison term; rehabilitated.

KALLIO Urho, 1899–?; b. Finland (brother of Lauri, same data); A-38.

KAJANDER Niilo, 1901–?; b. Viipurinl., Davidinp.; from Ohio, US 1931; Uhtua Kannussuo; A-17.

KALLIO Arvid, 1888–?; b. F. Turunl.; from US 1932; Vilga logger; A-11.

KANGAS Juho, 1890–1938; b. F. Vaasanl., Pekalank.; from Canada 1934; A-22.

KAREN Kalle, 1899–?; b. F. Jyväskylä; from Vancouver, Canada, 1932; Keretsk sawmill; A-5.**

KARHU Juho, 1891–38; b. F. Vaasanl., Lehmijoki; from Warren, Ohio 1931; Kondopoga Sunastroi; A-38.**

KARI Iivar, 1890–1938, from Duluth, Minn. 1931; Kondopoga paper mill; P-17.**

KARI Frans, 1889–1938; b. F. Oulunl., Patijoki; from Astoria, Oregon 1931; Petrozavodsk ski factory; P-3.**

KASKI Johan-Edward, 1879–?; b. Finland; from Cobalt Canada 1932; Aunus district, "Säde"; A-38.

KATAJA Arvo, 1898–1938; b. Turku-Porinl., Kiurola; from Ontario Canada 1932; P-13.**

KAUPPI (Kauppinen) Emil, 1884–1938; b. F. Kotka; from Warren, Ohio, US 1932; Petrozavodsk Onegaa plant; P-16.**

KAUPPI Theodor (Teddy), 1919–1938; b. N.H., US; Petrozavodsk musician; A-34.**

KESANTO Uuno son of Martti (Ap.-1), 1917–?,(a 10-year sent.); b. US, from US 1932; Kiestinki, a teacher; A-8.

KESKIAHO Aarne, 1898–?; b. Finland; from Canada 1932; Kondopoga paper mill; P-2.

KESKINEN Axel, 1882–1938; b. Finland; from Canada 1932; Uhtua logger.P-8.*

KETOLA Niilo, 1907–?; b. F. Turku-Porinl.; from Canada 1931; Matrosa; A-15.

KINNUNEN Kaarlo, 1881–?; b. Finland; from Canada, and sons

KINNUNEN Ilmari, 1913–?; b. Norway, from Canada 1931; A-15

KINNUNEN Niilo, 1905–?; b. Norway; from Canada 1931; A-16.

KINNUNEN Olli, 1914–?, b. Oulunl., Kuhmonen; from Canada; Oleneostrovsk; A-8;

KIVISTÖ August, 1905–?;l b. F. Vaasanl., Kauhava; from US 1932; Petrozavodsk ski factory; A-12.

KOISTINEN Erkki, 1906–?; b. Finland;; from Canada 1933; Matrosa tractor driver; A-9.

KOIVUMÄKI Eino, 1901–?; b. F. Turunl., Tykkö; from Toronto, Canada 1932; Vilga; A-12.

KOLHONEN Eino, 1899–?; b. F. Viipurinl., Kolhana; from Canada 1934; Uhtua, Kannussuo; A-18.

KOLEHMAINEN David, 1881–?; b. Finland; from US 1931; Kondopoga Sunastroi; A-38.

KORHONEN Elmer, son of Wäinö (see App.-1) 1915–?; b. Sacramento, Cal.; from US in 1932; Petrozavodsk, electrician. A-38.

KORPOLA Edward, 1905–?; b. F. Vaasanl.; from US 1933; A-11.

KOSKELA Viktor-Albin, 1901–? (among the 62 whose sentence was "commuted"); b. F. Vaasanl., Alauksenp.; from US 1930; Petrozavodsk painter, P-2.*

KOSKINEN Tuomas, 1908–?; b. F. Vaasanl.; from Canada 1932; Kondopoga carpenter; A-13.

KUJALA Rudolf Jaakko's son, 1916–?; b. US; from US 1933; Petrozavodsk Karelavto; A-38.

KUJALA Jaakko Jaakko's son, 1895–?; b. Finland; from US 1932; Petrozavodsk Karelavto; A-38.

KUKKO Albin, 1888–?; b. Finland (?); from Port William, Canada 1931; Matrosa, logger; A-38.

KULMALA Arvik, 1887–1938; b. Finland; from Canada 1931; Uhtua stableman; P-13.*

KULMALA Johan, 1895–1938; b. Vaasanl. Kurikko; from Cobalt Canada 1931; Petrozavodsk ski factory; P-17.

KUPIAS Viljo, 1902–1938, b. F. Viipurinl.; from Canada 1931; Ondozero, logger; P-11.*

KUUSELA Vilho, 1908–?; b. F. Alavesi; from Canada 1932; Petrozavodsk ski factory; P-2.* (death sent. was commuted, no further info).

KYTÖMÄKI Kalle, 1890–?; b. F. Vaasanl.; from Canada 1931; Matrosa logger; A-15.

LAAKKONEN Juho-Jalmari. 1900–1938; b. F. Kuopio; from Canada 1932; Petrozavodsk lumber yard; P-16.**

LAHTI Kalle, 1908–?; b. F. Ulvila; from Gardner, Mass. 1931; A-36.

LAHTI Otto, 1890–ret. and died in an Old Folks' Home; from US 1931; Matrosa, logger; A-37.

LAINE Erkki, 1899–?; b. F. Viipurinl; from US 1932; Kondopoga Suna sawmill; A-26.

LAHTI Eugene, 1919–?; b. US, Ohio; from Ashtabula, Ohio 1931; Petrozavodsk painter; A-38.

LAIHO Antti (Anton),1885–?; b. F. Turunl.; from Keene, NH 1932; Pai tractor station; A-6.**

LAINE Toivo, 1900–?; b. F. Oulunl., Karhula; from Canada 1932; Petrozavodsk lumber storage; A-14.

LAINE Wilho (Enoch), 1901–?; b. F. Hämeenlinna, Antinniemi; from US 1933; Pryazha logging camp instructor; A-5.

LAITI Pauli, 1884–?; b. F. Kuopio; from US 1933; Kannussuo, logger; A-18.

LAITILA Walter, 1905–?; b. F. Vaasanl., Jalosjärvi; from US 1931; Petrozavodsk driver; A-38. **

LAITINEN Juho, 1895–?; b. Helsinki; from US 1931; Petrozavodsk, electrician; A-38.

LAMPINEN Risto, 1885–?; b. F. Vaasanl. Alavanp.; from US 1931; Kiestinki Chernov logging camp; P-10.*

LAUKKANEN Lauri, 1884–?; b. F. Vaasanl. Alavus; from US 1931; Rugozero bookshop; A-6.

LAUTALA Fanni, 1894– released in 1943; from US 1932; Kiestinki; A-8.**

LEHTI Kalle, 1904–1938; b. F. Hämeenl., Kustaanp.; from Waukegan, Ill.1932; Uhtua, Kannussuo; P-11.

LEHTINEN Arthur, 1897–?; b. Finland; A-3 (?)

LEHTO John (Juho), 1882–?; b. F. Viipurinl.; from US 1932; Petrozavodsk ski factory; A-32.

LEHTO Kalle Viktor's son, 1895–?; b. Finland; from Canada 1932; Velikaya Guba, sawmill; A-5.

LEHTONEN August, 1891–1938; b. Hämeenl., Valkeakoski; from Canada 1933; Kondopoga; P-14.**

LEHTONEN Kalle, 1904–1938; b. Finland; from Mich.1931; Vilga mechanic; A-2.

LEHTONEN Oskar, 1892–1938; b. F. Uudenmaanl.; from Canada 1931; Petrozavodsk ski factory; P-4.

LEINO Leo, 1882–?; b. Finland, from Aberdeen, Wash. 1923; "Kylväjä", then Petrozavodsk museum; A-7.

LEINO Viktor, 1917–?; b. New York; from US 1931; Petrozavodsk ski factory; A-34.

LEINONEN Mesi-Pertti, 1894–?; b. F. Oulunl. Alanka; from US 1931; Petrozavodsk welder; A-38.

LEINONEN Hilja, 1905–?; b. Finland; (supposition: wife of Leivonen/Leivonen Karl, see App.-1); Kondopoga construction; P-3.*

LEPISTÖ Jaakko, 1985–1938; b. F. Vaasanl. Lapua; from Nashwauk, Minn. 1931; Tunkua-Pai. logger; A-8.**

LEPPÄ Alma, 1886–1938; b. F. Kuopuionl.; from US 1932; Matrosa; P-4.*

LEPPÄLÄ August, 1887–1938; b. Finland; from US 1931; Kondopoga construction; P-3.*

LEPPÄNEN Hemmi, 1898–1938; b. Finland; from Canada 1932; Petrozavodsk ski factory; P-16.*

LIND Tauno, 1913–1938; b. F. Oulunl, Kaukipudas; arrival(?);P-12.*

LINDROOS Julius, 1898–1938; b. F. Turku-Porinl.; from US 1932; Kondopoga brick factory; P-2.

LINNANMäKI Aleksi, 1890–?; b. F. Vaasanl., Alapiiri; from Canada 1934; Losinaya Gora, logger; A-14.

LISTRÖM (Lindström) Wäinö, 1900–?; b. Finland, Venkuja; from Canada 1932; Aunus Ilyinsky state farm; A-38.

LÖNN Albert, 1911–1985(?), b. US; from Detroit, Mich. 1932; Petrozavodsk-Suojärvi, (See "R.E." p.p.167–170); A-38.**

LUOMA Axel, 1888–?; b. F. Vaasanl. Lieteenpohjank.; from US 1931; Padozero logger; A-21.

LUND Wäinö, 1899–?; b. F. Vaasa; from US in 1931; Petrozavodsk worker; P-27.** His wife Sally LUND was a well-known poet in Karelia.

LYYTINEN Veikko, 1910–?; b. F. Kuopionl. Varposti; from Canada 1934; Uhtua Kannussuo, blacksmith; A-18.

MÄKELÄ Kalervo, 1919–1939; b. Ishpeming, US; from US 1931; Petrozavodsk, musician; P-4.**

MÄKELÄ Nestor, 1897–?; b. F. Vaasanl. Koivisto; from Canada 1932; Padany logger; A-20.

MÄKI Allan, 1917–1938; b. US; from US 1927; "Työ", then Onega plant; P-17. His brother:

MÄKI Eugene, 1919–?; b. US; from US 1927; same; P-16—a 10-year sentence;

MÄKI Emil; 1887–1938; b. F. Hämeenl., Heltaniemi; from Canada 1932; Uhtua carpenter; P-2.**

MÄKI Kerttu, 1901–?; b. F. Mikkelinl.; from US 1927; "Työ", then Karelia; A-38.

MÄKI Lauri Karl's son; 1912–?; b. US; from US 1934; Uhtua logger; A-7.

MÄKI Oscar, 1889–?; b. Finland; from US 1931; Kondopoga paper mill; A-32.

MÄKI (Hill) Oscar, 1888–1938; b. F. Turunl.; from Canada 1931; Uhtua, Kannussuo; P-4.

MÄKI Victor, 1896–1938; F. Merikorvenl., Yläkyla; might be from Finland; Kandalaksha; P-6.

MÄKI (Mäkipräsi) Pauli, 1906–?; b. F. Vaasanl.; from Canada 1932; Petrozavodsk electrician; A-38.

MÄKI Pekka, 1885–1938; b. Finland; from US 1931; Kondopoga office worker; P-3.*

MAKKONEN Kalle, 1898–?; b. F. Viipuri; from US 1932; Matrosa, logger; A-15.

MÄKYNEN John, 1993–?; b. f. Lapuanl. Hermanninp.; from Sudbury, Canada 1933; Vilga power station; A-10.**

MANNER Walter, 1937–living; b. Port Chester, NY; Petrozavodsk musician; A-36.**

MATTSON Toivo, 1901–?; b. F. Vaasanl. Karstila; from Vancouver Canada 1932; Vilga road builder; A-10.

MERILÄ Leonard, 1886–1938; b. F. Oulunl. Kirkko; from Grand Rapids, Mich. 1931; Petrozavodsk carpenter; A-6.**

MESI Arvo, 1890–1938; b. F. Uusimaa; from US 1931; Petrozavodsk musician; P-2.

METSÄPURO (Metsäpelto) William-Edward,1904–1938; b. F. Vaasanl., Lapua; from Canada 1934; Tumba logger; P-8.*

MIKKILÄ Juho, 1905–?; b. F. Vaasanl., Hirvijoki; from Canada 1931; Vilga power station; A-9.

MIKKONEN Marie, 1918–1993; b. F. Pollakkala; from US 1934; Petrozavodsk music teacher; P-17—a 10-year sent. was cancelled.** Her father

MIKKONEN Kalle was arrested and returned after 10 years of camps. No information documented.**

MOISIO Aleksi, 1930–1938; b. F. Hämeenlinna; from US 1930; Petrozavodsk musician; P-2.**

MURTO Pentti, 1916–?; b. Mich. US; from US 1933; Petrozavodsk electrician.A-38.**

MUSTONEN Oskar, 1896–?; b. F. Turunl., Sotkamo; from Canada 1932; Matrosa logger; A-15.

MUURIAISNIEMI Wäinö, 1905–?; b. Finland; from Canada 1932; Uhtua Kannussuo, cashier; A-17.

MYLLYLÄ Esa, 1897–1938; b. F. Oulunl. Nivalanp.; from Canada 1931; Petrozavodsk ski factory; P-3.*

MYLLYNIEMI John, 1897–?; b. Finland; from Brookston, Minn. 1931; Uhtua cashier; A-30.

NAHKALA John (Juho), 1983–?; b. F. Oulunl., Sikajoki; from Angora, Minn.1931; Kondopoga paper mill; A-17.

NELSON Cecelia, 1915–1995; b. Newberry, US; from US 1934; Petrozavodsk music school, A-33, first 10-year sent., then released almost immediately.**

NENONEN Arnold, 1914–1938; b. US, from Pittsburg, Penn. 1933; Petrozavodsk musician; P-4.**

NIEMI Albert, 1885–1938; b. Finland; from US 1932; Kondopoga paper mill, locksmith; P-11.

NIEMI August, 1877–?; b. US; from US in 1932; Uhtua; from Corgan's file: Niemi was sentenced to 10 years.

NIEMI Esther, 1902–?; b. Duluth, Minn.; from US 1931; Kondopoga paper mill; A-14. Sent. commuted to 8 years.

NIEMI Johan, 1906–1938; b. F. Oulunl., Sikajoki; from Canada 1931; Kannussuo, mechanic. P-5.

NIEMI Kristian 1893–1938; b. Finland; from Longviews, Wash. 1932; Lososinnoye; A-13.

NIEMI Wäinö, 1895–1938; b. F. Turunl., Korvianp.; from US 1932; Petrozavodsk car mechanic; P-16.

NIINISALO Samuel,1893–?; b. F. Uudenmaanl. Espoo; from Canada 1932; Vilga carpenter; A-9. (See Ch."War" about his son).

NIITTYNEN Karl, 1895–?; b. F. Vaasanl. Saarijärvi; from Canada 1931; Kondopoga paper mill; A-12.

NIKANDER Victor, 1892–?; b. Uudenmaanl, Nurmijärvi; from Canada 1931; Petrozavodsk Karelavto; P-27, a 10-year sent.

NIVA Emil, 1882–1938; b. Oulunl., Kalajoki; from S.Dakota 1931; Padozero carpenter; A-1 & 12.**

NORLUND Viktor, 1900–?; b. F. Hämeenl.Pirkkola; from Canada 1931; Uhtua agronomist; A-6.

NOUSIAINEN Elmer, 1913–living; b. US; from Daisytown, Penn.; 8 years in a gulag and then mandatory settlement; Petrozavodsk musician; not in the books.**

NURMI Jalmari, 1901-?; b. Finland; from Canada 1931; A-14.

NURMI Kustaa,1881–?; b. Finland; from Kirkland Lake, Canada, 1930; Petrozavodsk ski factory; A-7

NYLANDER Sander (Santtu?) 1895–?; b. F. Kotka; from Brit.Columbia, Canada 1931; Kondopoga paper mill; A-15.

NYLUND Nikolai, 1906–?; b. Finland; from Canada 1931; Vonganperä logger; A-16.

OINONEN Eino, 1906–?; b.?; from Cloquet, Minn. 1932; Kondopoga, Lenlesstroi; A-9.

OJALA Wäinö, 1904–1938; b. Finland; from Canada 1931; Chirka-Kemi; P-5.

OLKINUORA Armas, 1902–?; b. F. Viipurinl., Kuhkola; from US 1931; Pryazha mechanic; A-12.

PAANANEN Walter, 1891–1938; b. F. Vaasanl., Purvola; from Mass. US 1930; Petrozavodsk ski factory.**

PÄIVINEN Yrjö 1903–?; b. Finland; from Canada 1931; Uhtua administrator of National theater; A-14.

PARTANEN Emil, b. F. Helsinki; 1895–?; from Canada 1932; (died in post-war years in Pai); Matrosa-Pai, logger; A-38.

PELTOLA Einari, 1901–1938; b. F. Viipurinl., Virelä; from Hoaquim Wash. 1931; Vilga logger; P-11.

PESONEN Felix, 1895–?; b. F. Viipurinl. Valkeala; from US 1931; Lososinnoye logger; A-10.

PITKÄSALO Emil, 1902–?; b. F. Vaasanl., Särki; from Canada 1930; Matrosa tractor driver; A-8.

POHJANSALO Antti-Jussi, 1880–1938; b. F. Kupionl., Lahdenk.; from Sudbury, Canada 1931; Kondopoga construction; P-27.**

PULKKA Elvira, 1918–1938; b. F. Kuopionl. Kannaslahti; from US; P-1.

PUUMALA Paavo, 1886–?; b. F. Kuopionl.; from Port William, Canada 1932; Petrozavodsk lumber yard; A-28—returned after a 3-year sentence.**

PUUSTINEN Emil, 1890–1938; b. Finland; from Long Isl, NY 1932; Interposyolok; P-17.**

PYYHKÖNEN Juho, 1889–?; b. Finland; from Canada 1932; A-12.

RAISIO Iivari, 1894–?; b. F. Vaasanl. Alavus; from Canada 1932; Kannussuo logger; A-18.

RAISIO (Raivio) Ida, 1892–?; from US 1932; homemaker; P-16 death sent. commuted to 10 of imprisonment.

RANTA Antti, 1896–?; b. F. Oulunl. Liminkä; from Canada 1931; Vilga, carpenter; A-10.

RANTA Antti, 1898–1938. b. Finland; no mention of where he arrived from, Rugozero logger; P-A-145.

RANTAKALLIO Iivari, 1899–?; b. F. Viipurinl., Kuopionk.; from US 1931; Uhtua communal services; A-177.

RANTA Wäinö 1888–?; b. F. Turunl., Eurank.; from Canada 1932; Uhtua Kannussuo logger; A-17. (See Ch."War").

RANTANIEMI Toivo, 1906–?; b. F. Vaasanl.; from US 1934; Uhtua carpenter; A-16.

RAUHALA Tauno, 1915–living; b. F. Ylitaro; from Warren, Ohio 1932; Petrozavodsk power station; A-38.

RAUTAVIRTA Yrjö, 1897–1938; b. F. Vaasanl. Teuvonk.; from Canada 1932; P-4.

RAUTIO Antti, 1909–?; b. Finland (?); from US 1931; A-11.

RINNE Ville, 1906–?; b. F. Vaasanl., Peltoniemi; from Canada 1931; Matrosa logger; A-14.

RINNE Kalle, 1894–?; b. F. Forsa; from Canada 1931; Petrozavodsk mechanic; A-26.

RINTALA Toivo, 1904–?; b. F. Vaasanl., Pyntyrä; from Canada 1934; A-7.

RISTINEN Uuno 1911–?; b. F. Vaasanl. Maltink.; from Canada 1932; Kannussuo logger. A-18.

RITARI Wilho, 1882–?; b. F. Vaasanl.; from Canada 1933; Vilga mechanic; A-11.

ROINE Reino, 1907–?; b. US; from US 1931; Petrozavodsk Karelavto; A-38.

ROSENGREN Arthur, 1904–?; b. F. Turunl. Pekkalank.; from US 1933; Uhtua Kannussuo; P-5.

RUOHOMAA Heikki, 1904–1938; b. Finland; from US 1932; Tikhi Navolok logger; P-26.

SAARENKANTA Wäinö, 1893–?; b. F. Turku-Porinl, Vasunti; from Canada 1932; Padany, Tumba lumber camp; A-21.

SAARENPÄÄ Solomon, 1881–1938; from US; Kiestinki; A-1 & file 79—executed.

SALMAN (Selman) Juho, 1888–1938; b. F. Euramäki; from US 1931; Petrozavodsk ski factory; P-27.

SALMI William, 1894–1938; b. Finland; from US 1931; Kondopoga construction; P-2.

SALMI Yrjö, 1895–1938; b. Finland; from Waukegan Ill, 1931; Petrozavodsk construction; A-12.**

SALMINEN Alpo. 1916–?; b. F. Turunl., Kutunankanp.; from Canada 1932; Uhtua, Kannussuo; A-22.

SALMINEN Eino, 1901–1938; F. Tattari Nikkilänp.; from Chicago, ILL. 1931; Petrozavodsk construction; A-5.**

SALMINEN Eino, 1906–?; b. F. Lapinl., Ruono; from US 1931; Uhtua National theater actor; A-17.

SALMINEN Juho, 1890–1938; b. Finland; from Canada 1930; Kondopoga Lenstroi; P-3.

SALMINEN Oiva, 1912–1938; B. US Crystal Falls; from US 1931; Petrozavodsk, Onega plant; P-17.

SALMINEN Richard, 1883–?; b. F. Vaasanl., Keula; from US 1932; Svyatnavolok school janitor; A-12

SALO Arthur, 1991–?; b. F. Turunl., Laitilanp.; from Mich.US 1931; Lososinnoye tractor team; P-27. Death sent. commuted for a 10-year sent.

SALO Rafael, 1894–?; b. F. Turku; from Canada 1932; Uhtua; A-19.

SALO Simo (Simeon), 1890–1938; b. Finland; from Detroit, Mich.1931; Petrozavodsk construction; A-15.**

SALOKAARI (Salokari) Leo, 1902–1938; from Canada 1931; Petrozavodsk ski factory; P-16.

SALONEN Emil, 1896–1938; b. F. Tampere; from US 1932; Uhtua; P-27.**

SALONEN Toivo, 1904–?; b. F. Turunl., Jyytelä; from US; Uhtua. Indication of arrest in Corgan's file.

SANKARI Lempi, 1902–?; b. F. Turunl.Augustat; from Canada 1931; Matrosa, power station; A-15.**

SEPPÄLÄ Oskari, 1904–?; b. F. Vaasanl.; from Canada 1931; Matrosa; A-11.

SEPPÄLÄ Wainö, 1900–1938; b. F. Uudenmaanl.; from Canada 1932; Uhtua Kannussuo; P-5.

SEPPÄNEN Ilmari, 1903–1938, b. Finland; from America; Kondopoga logging; P-12.

SIIKKI Olavi, 1916–1939; b. Detroit, Mich.; from US 1930; Petrozavodsk music school. P-17.**

SILLANPÄÄ Wester, 1899–?; b. F. Vaasanl., Kirkonk.; from US in 1933; Lososinnoye, blacksmith; A-15.

SILLANPÄÄ Hulda, 1892–?; b. Canada; from Canada; A-16—a 10-year sentence.

SILVAN Wäinö, 1916–?; b. US; from US in 1933; Uhtua logger; A-13.

SIREN Hank (John), 1915–living?; b. Duluth, Minn.; from US 1932; Kondopoga paper mill electrician; A-12.**

SOINI Wäinö, 1890–?; b. F. Virtani Urasten(?); from Sugar Isl,. Mich. 1931; Belomorsk district, Kochkoma logger; A-8.

SOMPPI (Somppimäki) Gustav, 1892–1938; b. F. Vaasanl.; from Canada 1932; P-2.

SORVALI Armas, 1904–1938; b. F. Viipurinl., Säkkijärvi; from Canada 1931; Rugozero,office worker; P-5; his wife:

SORVALI Tyyne, 1909–1938; b. Turunl., Henkilahti; from Canada 1931;Rugozero, printing house; P-10.

SPANGER Juho, 1891–?; b. Finland; from Canada 1931; Petrozavodsk electrician; A-38.

STARK Ivan (John), 1906–?; b. F. Ilmajoki; from Canada 1932; Lososinnoye logger; A-2.

STENFORS Eino, 1902–?; b. F. Turku-Porinl.; from Cobalt, Canada 1927; Aunus "Säde", then Matrosa; A-14.

STROM Olga-Marie, 1885–?; b. Finland; from Milford, NH 1934; Uhtua Children's home worker; A-35—a 10-year sent.

STROM Norman (Harmon) 1912–?; b. Canada; from Canada 1931; Matkachi sanatorium painter; A-11.

SUNI Juho (John), 1892–?; b. F. Vaasanl. Vuortamaan p.; from US 1931; Petrozavodsk, Karelavto; A-38.

SWORD Ansa, 1919–1938; b. US; from US 1931, Petrozavodsk musician; P-4.

TAIPALE Leo, 1913–?; b. Finland Andria; from Canada 1931; Petrozavodsk Onega plant, constructor; A-8.

TAKKO Wäinö, 1888–?; b. F. Viipurinl. Telikkala; from Canada 1926; Aunus "Säde"; A-6.

TAMMINEN Karl, 1902–1938; b. Finland; from Canada 1931; Pai; P-A-145.

TAMMINEN Matti, 1901–?; b. F. Forssa; from Canada 1932; Kem district, Avneporog; A-10.

TAMMINEN Sulo, 1893–1938; b. F. Turku-Porinl., Kirkonk.; from Chicago 1931; Pai; P-11.

TARVAINEN Hjalmar, 1889–1938; b. F. Vaasanl. Suovalahti; from Conneaut, Ohio 1931; Kondopoga paper mill; A-19.**

TIHKARI Oskari, 1886–?; b. F. Helsinginl.; from US; Matrosa logger; A-13.

TIIAINEN Matti, 1906–?; b. F. Sortavala; from Kirkland Lake, Canada; worked in Sortavala; A-38. Reported missing in war since 1945. His brother:

TIIAINEN Pauli, 1904–?;b. Finland; "came to Russia with parents in 1915" (?), biology teacher at a Teachers' college in Petrozavodsk. A-12.

TOHKA Otto, 1891–1938; b. F. Viipurinl., Valkeala; from Canada 1934; Kondopoga paper mill; A-6.

TOLONEN Lempi David's daughter (see app.-1); 1930–living; b. Webster's Corner, Canada; from Canada 1932; Vilga; not registered in books; see "R.E." p.p.111.**

TORNIAINEN Emil, 1891–1938; b. Finland; from Canada 1931; Kondopoga paper mill; P-3.

TUISKU Eino, 1897–?; b. F. Vaasanl.; from US 1931; Vilga blacksmith; A-11.

TUOMELA Keijo, 1921–1938; b. Mass., US; from US 1932; Petrozavodsk music school student; P-2.**

TUOMINEN Hannu, 1905–?; b. F. Oulunl.; from Canada 1932; Uhtua Kannussuo; A-18.

TUOMINEN Heikki, 1900–?; b. F. Vaasanl., Himanganp.; from Canada 1932; Petrozavodsk ski factory A-15.

TUOMINEN Konsta, 1901–1938; b. Finland; from US 1931; Kondopoga logging; P-27.

TURUNEN Toivo, 1912–?; b. F. Turunl, Kisankoski; from US 1931; Petrozavodsk painter; A-5.

TUULOS Nikki, 1899–?; b. F. Kotka; from Cobalt, Canada 1927; Aunus, "Säde"; A-18.

UUSITALO Jalmari, 1885–1938; b. F. Vaasanl. Isojoki, Peurala;; from America 1922; Uhtua "Säde", P-17.

UUTELA Emil, 1890–?; b. F. Viipurinl. Hirvelä; from Mass.US 1932; Vilga blacksmith; A-10.**

WAGLUND Eino, 1927–1938; b. F. Turku-Porinl., Kaukkola; from US 1922; Pyazhievän Selkä, mechanic; P-18.

VÄHÄKANGAS Toivo, 1902–1938; b. F. Oulunl., Raaha; from Canada 1932; Rukaj arvi logger; A-36.

VAHALA (Vanhala) Jalmari. 1883–?; b. F. Turku-Porinl. Papalank.; from US 1932; Petrozavodsk Karelavto; A-38.

VÄHKÄRI Oskari, 1900–?; b. F. Oulunl., Tervola; from America, 1931; Vilga logger; A-2.

WAHLROS Paavo, 1905–?; b.New York; from US 1930; Petrozavodsk, Onega plant; A-38; His brother:

WAHLROS Kaarlo; 1902–1938; US. everything the same but: worked at Vilga. rehabilitated in 92/2.

VÄIHKELÄ Tauno, 1905–?; b. F. Mikkelinl., Joutsi; from Canada 1932; Uhtua driver; A-25.

VAINIO Väinö, 1889–?; b. F. Nastola; from Canada; Petrozavodsk ski factory; A-36.

VÄKEVÄ Toivo, 1906–1939; b.Canada; from Canada 1931; construction manager; P-A-142.

VALKONEN Hugo, 1896–?; b. F. Viipurinl., Urpola; from Canada 1931; Vilga, road builder; A-10.

VALLIN (Wallen) August, 1878–?; b. F. Nivajärvi; from US 1930; Kondopoga, Sandal; A-10.

WALLEN Emil, 1883–1938; b. F. Pori; from America 1932; Aunus mechanic; P-27.

VALO Alma, 1895–?; b. F. Viipurinl., Hirvelä; from US 1932; Petrozavodsk, homemaker; A-38.

VALTONEN Aarne, 1911–1938; b.US, Gilbert Minn.; from Conneticut 1932; Kondopoga ambulance driver. P-4.

VÄRJÄ August, 1897–?; b. F. Kuusenkoski; from Canada 1931; Interposyolok; A-4.

VÄRJÄ Martti, 1891–?; b. Kymeenranta; from Canada 1933; Interposyolok; A-2.

WEBSTER Elmer, 1892–?; b. F. Vaasanl.; from Canada 1932; Petrozavodsk stonecutter; A-38.

WENDELIN Eino-Edward, 1899–?; b. Hogfors(?); from Toronto, Canada 1931; Petrozavodsk Onega plant; A-36.

VIIJALA (Viala) Juho (Eino), 1903–?; b. F. Turunl., Valjakkala; from Canada 1932; Vilga blacksmith; A-10.

WIITANEN Kalle (Charles), 1877–?; b. F. Turunl., Villilä; from Cloquet, Minn. 1931; Kem carpenter; P-15.

VIITANIEMI Verner, 1897–1938; from US 1931; Petrozavodsk, Onega plant; P-16.**

VIITASALO Lauri, 1909–1938; b. F. Vaasanl., Viitasalonk.; from Canada 1934; Losinaya Gora. A-24 written in hand "died Sept.7, 1938".

WIKSTRÖM Einari, b.Helsinki, from S.Porcupine, Canada 1932; Matrosa; A-7. He returned after a 20-year absence. See "R.E.", p.p. 84–85.

VIRONEN Karl, 1882–?; b. F. Kuopiuonl., Vesamäki; from Canada 1927; Uhtua Kis-Kis logging camp; A-21.

VIRTANEN Ivan (John) 1893–1938; b. F. Hiterjoki (?); from US 1932; Petrozavodsk ski factory; P-2.

VUORI Jaakko, 1912–?; b. Africa, US; from US 1932; Kem district Avneporog, tractor driver; A-3.

VUORI Jaakko, 1894–1938; b. F. Vaasanl., Ämmälä; from New York 1932; Aunus, Ilyinsky state farm; P-27.

VUORIMAA (Vuorenmaa) Selma, 1898–? b. Viipuri; from Canada 1931; Vilga; P-4. A 10-year sentence. In her paper: "Husband arrested in Vilga"—no papers on him. Evidently it is:

VUORIMAA (Vuorenmaa) Edward—same arrival date.

YLINEN Paul, 1915–? but he returned; b. F. Turunl.; from Ludlow, Vermont 1931; A-38.

YLITALO Jaakko, 1898–?; b. F. Vaasanl. Pouttola; from US 1926; Karelian Teachers' college, worker. Before that "Kylväjä" and state farm N 2; A-9.

YRJÖLÄ Pekka, 1888–?; b. F. Viipurinl., Kukkola; from US 1931; Kondopoga Sunsstroi; A-38.

The total N of victims from Albums and Protocols 325. Among them:

men	306
women	19
arrivals from the USA	177
arrivals from Canada	142
unknown where they are from	6

The following women are among the returnees: Dahlberg, Erkkilä, Haakana, Lautala, Mikkonen, Nelson. They returned to their families but have passed on.

APPENDIX 4.

Information on illegal arrests received from family or close friends (Those who had received rehabilitation papers in the period of the Khrushschev "thaw").

ANTTILA Toivo, 1909–1938; from Aurora Mich.

BJÖRN Sulo, b.1910, Minn., US; from US 1932.

BJÖRNINEN Otto, b. Finland, from Michigan in 1931, Petrozavodsk national theater.

BRUNILA Wilho, 1903–?; b. F. Kyminl., from Canada 1932; Kondopoga brick factory. A-2.

COPPER Allan, b. US; from New York 1932; Petrozavodsk.

COPPER Sally (his sister); b. US; from New York 1932; Petrozavodsk.

ERNEST Kalle; b. ?; from Minn., US 1932; Matrosa.

FAGER-MÄKELÄ Tauno, b.1914–1938, b. US, from Quincy Mass. 1932.

FORSTEN John, from Cleveland, Ohio, 1931. Returned from prison.

GILBEREG Theodor, from Cleveland, Ohio 1930; Uhtua.

GRANDEL Wäinö (see app.N 2, son Toivo); from Detroit, Mich.1933.

HAATAJA Wäinö, from Timmins, Canada.

HARTOLA Jussi, from Canada 1931.

HENDRICKSON Oscar and son Tauno (the fact of Tauno's death has not been established—war or LC); to Russia in 1923, see "R.E., p.p. 59–60).

HILL Urho, 1884–1938; b. Finland; from Canada 1933. Petrozavodsk ski factory.

HILTUNEN Yrjö; from Canada 1931. (Wife Ida, daughter Anne).

HIRVONEN Eino; from Duluth, Minn.; returned after 8 years of prison.

HONKA Paavo, b. Finland; from Detroit, Mich. 1931; Petrozavodsk.

HUUSKONEN Abel, from Sebeka, Minn. 1931.

INKINEN Donald, 1910–1938; b. US; from Detroit, Mich.1931. Petrozavodsk.

ISOLA Matti, 1888–1938; b. Finland; from Ipswich, NH, US 1933. Petrozavodsk.

JAAKKOLA Aarne 1911–1938; from Detroit, Mich., 1933. Nephew of the Klemola's (see app.2).

JASKAR Wäinö; from Ontario, Canada, 1931; Matrosa.

JERMILÄ Wäinö, 1898–1938; from Canada 1931; Matrosa.

JOHNSON Kalle; from Cleveland Ohio.

JOHNSON Risto; from Waukegan, Ill. 1932; Kylväjä..

JUNTUNEN Kalle, 1884–1938; from Detroit, Mich. 1932; Uhtua.

KANNINEN Yrjö; from Peabody, Mass.

KAUPPI Onni Sr.; from Long Island, NY. (Onni Jr. living in Russia. See "R.E.", p.77).

KEMPPAINEN Kalle Sr., Arthur and Kalle Jr.; from Ladysmith, Canada. (See brother Axel in app.1).

KERTTULA Naimi, 1887–?; from Eben Junction, Mich.l 1932 (See Nestor, her husband, App.1).

KETOLA Iivari, 1899–?; from Sudbury, Canada 1931.** (See app.2—brother Niilo).

KILPINEN Lauri, 1897–?; from US in 1931; Aunus "Säde".

KOKKO Sulo and Pentti; from Canada in 1932.

KOSKI Uuno, 1914–1938; b. US; from New Jersey US 1932.

KOSKI Martha, 1938—returned after 8 years of imprisonment.

LAATUNEN Manu and his son

LAATUNEN Erkki, b.Windsor, Canada. Presumably living.

LÄHTEENOJA Vilho, 1899–?; from Canada in 1931.

LAHTI Sulo, his wife

LAHTI Ida and their son

LAHTI Wilfred,returned after incarceration, died in Petrozavodsk. (See "R.E." p.p.78–80).

LAHTI Kaisa from Detroit Mich.

LAINE Yrjö, his wife

LAINE Anna (returned after incarceration) and their daughter

LAHTI (Laine) Suoma. (See "R.E." p,p, 78–80).

LEHTIMÄKI Werner (see "R.E." p.p.95–98).

LEHTO Viktor, from Vancouver, Canada.

LEPISTÖ Hilarius, 1886–?; from Negaunee, Mich, 1933.

LEPISTÖ Eino, 1893–?, from Cobalt, Canada 1932.

LIND August from Detroit, Mich.; returned after a 10-year sentence.

LUOMA Alfred, 1877–1938; the family arrived from the State of Washington to "Kylväjä" in 1923. He figures in P-11.** All the family members but one, his wife, were arrested:

LUOMA William;

LUOMA Toivo (returned from incarceration);

LUOMA Aino;

LUOMA Sylvia (returned from incarceration);

LUOMA Elma (returned from incarseration).

MÄKI Edward from Mass. US in 1931 and his wife (?):

MÄKI Laura, who returned from prison.

MÄKI Wilho (Mäenpää William), from Vancouver, Canada 1932.

MÄYRÄ Jussi, from Ontario, Canada 1931.

METSÄLÄ Hugo, b. US, from Ontagonan, Mich. 1932.

METSÄPURO Paavo (Järvinen Eino), b. 1894 Tampere; from Maynard, Mass. 1932.

NIEMINEN Lauri-Jaakko, b. Hämeenlinna; from Ontario, Canada 1931; Interposyolok.

NISSEN (Nissinen) Conrad, from Windsor, Canada 1931.

NIXON Otto; from S.Dakota, US 1931; Interposyolok.

NORDEEN John from US.

OJALA Niilo, from Canada 1931.

OKKONEN Theodor from US and son

OKKONEN Olavi, b. US.

OLSON Oskar from US.

PEKKALA Kalle, 1888–?; from Maynard Mass. 1932; Suna state farm.

PIHJALA (Pihlaja) Oskar; from Canada 1931.

PILPPOLA Nestor; from US 1931.

RAJALA Louis, 1905–; from Waukegan Ill. 1931 (see "R.E." p.p. 124–128).

RANTA Eino, 1920–1938; b. Canada; from Canada 1932; Matrosa; P-A-141.

RANTA Elis, 1891–1938; b. Finland; from Monessen Penn. 1932.

RAUMA Edward, 1900–1938; from S.Dakota 1931.

RUOTSALA Lauri; from Owen, Wisc.

SALMELA Viljo, 1908–1938; from US 1931. (See "R.E." p.p.115–116).

SEPPÄNEN John, from Cloquet, Minn.1931.

STOLT Kalle Sr. (See "R.E.", p.122).

TISSARI-MILLER Emil, 1894–1938.

TOKO Väinö; Aunus, "Säde".

WARWICK Karl, from Port Chester, US, returned after incarceration, died in Karaganda.

TOTAL—86 Among them:	
men	77
women	9
from the US	52
from Canada	25

APPENDIX 5
WARTIME LABOR CAMP VICTIMS

(See "R.E." p.p.141–146. Some changes have occurred in the names and numbers. It remains extremely difficult to establish whether men perished in LC's or in action in 1941–1945. These are the results my efforts have yielded, including official inquiries to Republic Karelia's Prosecutor General offices. They are re-examining papers submitted by FSK. There are numerous LC-inmates from Finland, the USA and Canada who survived miraculously to tell their tragic stories. Without doubt this list does not cover all).

AHO Aate (Adi); b. 1885, Finland, Ähtäri; from Canada 1932.

AHO Ahti; b. Finland; from Canada 1932.

AHO Leo; b. Brantwood, WI.; from US 1933.

ALANEN Roy; b. US, Brookston, Minn.; from US 1931.

ALANEN Severi, from Port Arthur, Canada.

ANTTILA Toivo, from Palo, Minn.US.

ARVELA Asser; b. 1892, presumably in Finland; from Conneut, Ohio, US 1931.

DAHLMAN Tenho; b. US; from Montgomery, NY, US 1932.

DAHLSTRÖM Eino; b. 1888; from US 1931.

EDWIG Paul; b. US; from Portland, Oregon 1933.

EKLUND Emil; b. 1898; from Inwood, NY, US 1932.

HASALA Richard; b. US 1926; from Clifford, WI, US 1931.

HUHTAMO Karl; from Canada 1931.

JOKIMÄKI Ralph; b. 1922, Baraga, MI; from US 1931.

JUNELL Arvi; b. 1910; from Fairport, Ohio, US 1932.

JUVONEN Edwin; presumably US-born; from Detroit, MI 1933.

KAMPPI Yrjö; b. US, 1923; from Detroit, Mich. 1932.

KANGAS Eino; b. 1907; from Minn., US 1933.

KEMPPI Gideon Jr.; from Brit.Col., Canada 1932.

KEMPPI Eino, from Brit.Col., Canada 1932.

KETOLA Ahti; b. Calgary, Canada 1926; from Canada 1932.

KIVÄRI Kaarlo; b. Canada 1925; from Canada 1932.

KIVÄRI Kosti; b. Canada 1923; from Canada 1932.

KUUSELA Tuomas; b. Finland, 1888; from Markham, Mich.

LEHTINEN Matti; no other data. Information from his co-workers in Matrosa.

LEHTO Pekka; from Alberta, Canada.

LEIPÄLÄ Sam; b. Finland, 1896; from Fitchburg, Mass. 1932.

LINDSTEDT Wilho; b. 1910; from Canada 1931.

LUOMA Taisto; b. Canada 1923; from Canada 1932.

MÄKELÄ Oscar;(wife Hilma, son Roy); from Detroit, Mich. 1931.

MÄKI Aarne; from Kirkland Lake, Canada 1932.

MÄKI Juho; b. Finland 1889; from US 1931.

MARTTILA George; b. US; from Knife Falls, Minn.US 1931.

NIEMI George; b. US International Falls, Minn., US; from US 1932.

NIEMINEN David (wife Martha, daughter Ellen, both have died); from Detroit, Mich. 1932.

NORDLING Otto; from Canada 1931.

NYLANDER Henry; from Brit. Col., Canada 1931.

OJALA Iivari (family: Anna, Sarah, Eero); from State of Wash., US.

OJALEHTO Eino; from Baltimore, Maryland 1931.

PIHLAJAMÄKI Iisakki; b. 1903; from Detroit, Mich. 1932.

PRÄNNY Arvo-Johannes; from Ontario, Canada 1931.

RANTA (Rantamäki) Aarne; b. 1903; from Cobalt, Canada.

RANTA Kalle; b. 1893; from Detroit, Mich.1931.

RANTALA Oliver; b. 1918, US; from Bizbee, Arizona, US 1932.

RAUTIO Edwin; b. US Mich., 1922; from US 1932.

RINNE Sulo-Aarne; b. 1908; from Washington, DC 1933.

SAARI Eino; b. US, Brantwood, Wisc.; from US 1932.

SALMI Hannes; from Warren, Ohio, US 1932.

SALMINEN Kalle; from Chicago Ill., US.

SANDROS Sulo; b. Finland, Tampere, 1890; from Detroit, Mich.,US 1933.

SAVOLAINEN Wilho; b. Canada; from Canada 1931 and brother:

SAVOLAINEN Kauko; b. Canada; from Canada 1931.

SEPPÄNEN Eino; from Iron, Minn., US 1932.

STAHLBERG Toivo (wife Senja), from New York, US 1932.

TOIVONEN Taisto; b. US; presumably 1922; from Newberry, Mich. 1932.

VILKKILÄ Jussi; from Warren, Ohio.

VALLI (Pikkumäki) Tauno; b. Canada, 1922; from Kirkland Lake, Canada, 1932.

VALO Henry; b. 1900; from New York, US 1932.

VESA Arthur; from Green, Mich.US 1931.

VIRTANEN Wäinö; b. 1902 (?1899); from Port Arthur, Canada 1932.

WALLENIUS Kalle; (family: Eeva, Rauha, Aura); from Canada.

TOTAL 61 victims. Among them:

US-born	16
Canadian-born	8

TO THE READERS

Having read the pages you've certainly noticed the suppositions expressed concerning the fates of My People. I still harbor hopes that some may be found. I'd certainly appreciate any help you could offer. Here are a few names;

KETOLA Richard, b. 1915, Sudbury, Canada, son of Waino and Elsa; from Canada to Karelia in 1931. Close relatives are applying for information.

MERILAHTI Robert, b. 1915 (?), New York; from the US in 1931. Daughter Nelly and two grandchildren are cherishing the hope of hearing from him or about him. Nothing known since 1939.

MATTSON Aune, b.Worcester, Mass., 1920; from US in 1932 and

VALO Irene, b.New York, 1922; from US in 1932. Both these young ladies lost their parents in the purges and it is known that they made an attempt to get to their Homeland. Did they succeed? They were my personal friends too.

PITKANEN William, (b. In New York) last resting place and that of his parents, is in the Ural mountain region. Two daughters living in Russia are hoping to contact relatives living in the US.

HILTUNEN George, b. 1916, Rosegrave, Ontario, Canada, (he is in the picture on the cover page). Besides being an excellent scholar, he was a wonderful sportsman and artist. No information.

SUVANTO Into, b. circa 1912, Superior, Wisconsin. Inquiry of daughter.

Any information can be sent to the author:
1001 Clough Ave., Apt.215
Superior, Wisc. 54880.